Wordplay and Language Learning for Children

Wordplay and Language Learning for Children

Linda Gibson Geller
Queens College of the City University of New York

National Council of Teachers of English
1111 Kenyon Road, Urbana, Illinois 61801

Staff Editor: Lee Erwin

Book Design: Tom Kovacs for TGK Design

NCTE Stock Number 58218

Library of Congress Cataloging in Publication Data

Geller, Linda Gibson, 1938–
    Wordplay and language learning for children.

    Bibliography: p.
    1. Children—Language. 2. Play on words.
3. Language arts (Elementary) I. Title.
LB1139.L3G37 1985   372.6   85-18889
ISBN 0-8141-5821-8

Contents

Acknowledgments

I would like to extend special thanks to some of the many people who have made this book possible:

To Queens College of the City University of New York for granting released time to complete this manuscript (Faculty in Residence Award, 1984–85).

To *Language Arts* for permission to excerpt the following articles: "Riddling: A Playful Way to Explore Language" (September 1981); "Grasp of Meaning: Theory into Practice" (September 1982); "Children's Rhymes and Literacy Learning: Making Connections" (February 1983); and "Exploring Metaphor in Language Development and Learning" (February 1984).

To *Childhood Education* for permission to excerpt "A Verbal Gold Mine: Parody Play in the Classroom" (September/October 1982).

To Kay Gunderson for anecdotes from a classroom of three-year-olds, collected during her student internship at the Bank Street College of Education, New York City.

To the teachers of the Corlears School, New York City, who welcomed me into their classrooms to explore my ideas, and especially to Louise Crowe, Nancy Kline, and Betsy Elliot, colleagues whose insights, anecdotes, and samples of wordplay provided me with a steady source of material from the early childhood years.

Finally, to the children of the Corlears School, whose verbal play not only inspired but, in large part, created this monograph.

Introduction

Ladies and Gentlemen
I come before you
To stand behind you
To tell you what I know nothing about
Pull up a chair
And sit on the floor
Admission is free
Pay at the door.

My initiation into the world of elementary wordplay began when I was five years old. Up to that point, like most my age, I had been busily memorizing the ever-popular nursery rhymes. "Humpty-Dumpty," "Old King Cole," and many others were familiar figures. Images of these delightful, somewhat absurd beings were regularly evoked through repetitions—alone or with my kindergarten group—of the well-known verses. These rhythmical vignettes, however, were about to be displaced by the many and varied forms of traditional wordplay associated with the elementary ages. It was my brother, four years older than I, who was doing the initiating. I remember my first exposure to his repetition of "Ladies and Gentlemen / I come before you . . . etc." At the end, he laughed heartily and I attempted to figure out what it meant. My puzzled look only evoked a scathing "Dumb kid!" from my sophisticated sibling. At another time, I remember being introduced to one of the "moron" riddles: "Why," asked my brother, confident of my ignorance, "did the moron tiptoe past the medicine cabinet?" Silence from me, as expected. The punch line was delivered amid his guffaws: "So he wouldn't wake up the sleeping pills!" In the dark but hoping to be enlightened, I asked what "moron" meant. The answer came at a price—"A stupid kid! Like you, Stupid!"—and did not enlighten. It took a few more years before I was graced with understanding. I was brushing my teeth before bed, staring at the contents of the medicine cabinet, when light dawned. "*Sleeping* pills! . . . *Sleeping* pills!" I kept repeating amid giggles of delight, mixed with an awareness that, finally, I, too, had graduated to that place formerly reserved for "big kids" like my brother.

What I didn't know then was that I was simply following the path taken by most primary-age youngsters as they make the transition from babyhood to "kidhood." With this step comes exposure to a substantial repertoire of children's traditional wordplay. Initiation, then as now, takes place on the playground, through the sharing of newly learned examples, or, often, through the competitive repetitions of older siblings. During my elementary years, like most of my peers, I mastered a good portion of these items and repeated them with gusto at the appropriate moments. The end of the period brought an end to this kind of exploration and the moving on to other forms of play more closely allied with adult uses of humor. In between the toddler years and adolescence, nearly all youngsters explore an oral tradition in a way that is significant to both their language learning and their learning about the culture in which they live.

It was my work as a teacher of young children that prompted me to take a serious look at what appears a very nonserious activity. In school settings, we cannot ignore, even if we wished to, the many examples of humorous and playful language spontaneously as well as ritually exchanged among children. Not only do preschoolers bring a repertoire of nursery rhymes to their classrooms, but they often also break into spontaneous chants during their play. The use of rhymes and chants to choose an "it" or to accompany games begins in the primary grades and lasts through the middle elementary years. These years are also ones in which riddles, knock-knocks, and other joke forms make regular appearances on the playgrounds and in the halls and lunchrooms of our schools. The same is true of ritual insults and verses (e.g., "Roses are red / Violets are blue / If I looked like you / I'd live in a zoo"). In all of these categories of play, certain renditions receive endless airings for a period of time before they are dropped— only to be revived again by another group in another year. Indeed, I heard many of my current examples repeated a generation ago. Then, too, it is clear from recent books for children by Alvin Schwartz and Duncan Emrich that many of these same verbal vignettes have a long and "sacred" history, having served through the decades as frames for humorous, playful views of life.

For me, as an educator, the anomaly in this situation has been the absence of wordplay from the classroom—especially classrooms of the primary and middle elementary years. Teachers of these ages are aware of youngsters' penchant for play; however, most see no educational reason to bring it into the classroom. The question generally posed is, What does wordplay have to do with language education? or, more to the point: What does wordplay have to do with the teaching of reading and writing? In essence, these were the issues that prompted me to study the implications of children's wordplay for language learning. The question became: Does wordplay simply represent a momentary and incidental exploration of the absurd or does it have within it a systematic exploration of language and language functions? Research by psychologists, linguists, and educators confirms that children are not just "playing"; rather, they are learning much valuable information about how language works as they move from one form of play to another. In sum, it seems that between the toddler and adolescent years children move through discernible stages in their wordplay and that these stages are related to stages of language and literacy acquisition. Given these relations between play and language learning, it follows that wordplay activities are a potentially valuable resource to be included in language education programs for three- to eleven-year-olds.

My purpose, then, in writing this book is to elaborate the connections among language learning, language education, and children's wordplay. Each chapter examines some aspect of the interrelations between wordplay activities and the goals of language education. Because the book outlines the developmental course of these possibilities for children from three to eleven, it is divided into three sections. The first explores wordplay and language learning in the nursery years (three to four); the second the transition years (five to seven); and the last the middle elementary years (eight to eleven). Each section describes the linguistic forms and functions children tend to explore during those years. Play anecdotes and examples are taken from classroom observations and research. The anecdotes are meant to suggest ways of integrating wordplay and language education programs, and other suggestions for extending opportunities for play are offered in each section. Finally, because of what appears to be resistance to the idea of bringing such activities into the classroom—particularly middle elementary programs—relations between play and pedagogy are discussed in chapter 5.

The Nursery Years
(Three and Four)

1 Preschoolers and Speech Play

It is in early childhood programs that the idea of learning through play has had greatest acceptance; it is clear to teachers that children at these ages must participate in the choice and organization of their activities. Though teachers are needed to create the setting and to serve as models, guides, and/or protectors, children of three and four are the key initiators and shapers of much of their own learning.

Recently, language researchers have suggested that language acquisition derives from similar self-regulatory processes. During the preschool years, children move rapidly through successive phases of language learning, and it is generally agreed that by the time youngsters reach their fifth year the most challenging hurdles of language learning have been overcome. In Kornei Chukovsky's words ([1925] 1971), in their early years youngsters exhibit a kind of "linguistic genius"; they master intricate aspects of language forms and functions and become capable of carrying on fluent conversations with both peers and adults. This complex learning task, it should be remembered, is accomplished not just by a few; rather, all children, other than those with special physical or mental handicaps, become competent members of their community of speakers.

Teachers should take special note of the fact that this task is accomplished without benefit of direct instruction. Through regular exposure to language in use and through opportunities to use—and misuse—the system, children construct for themselves the nature of the code. They master complex structures of sound, meaning, and syntax without explicit descriptions of their many rules. Evidence of children's engagement in actively constructing the rules of the system is often revealed in their errors: for example, three-year-old Ben describes his contribution to preparing the class snack by saying, "I shaked the juice." Though Ben is correct in his choice of verb to express his action—it was frozen juice that had been put into a container for shaking with water—he used a form he's not likely to have heard before. Having not yet absorbed the irregular form "shook" into his language model, he employed the more common *-ed* rule governing the construction of past tense—a rule he has derived from his exposure to speech around him.

A similar example of inventive rule derivation is reported by Jean Berko Gleason (1967) in conversation with a four-year-old:

> *Child:* My teacher holded the baby rabbits and we patted them.
>
> *JBG:* Did you say your teacher held the baby rabbits?
>
> *Child:* Yes.
>
> *JBG:* What did you say she did?
>
> *Child:* She holded the baby rabbits and we patted them.
>
> *JBG:* Did you say she held them tightly?
>
> *Child:* No, she holded them loosely.

Like Ben, this child had learned the *-ed* rule for marking past tense. And though Gleason provided a model of the standard (again, irregular) form, the child persisted in the use of her own construction. Eventually, of course, these youngsters will revise their developing language models to incorporate irregular forms of *hold* and other verbs. What is remarkable in these and similar episodes is the developmental processes at work. Without exposure to mature language models, the child would not—in fact, could not—accomplish the task of learning to speak. Given the model, however, the child puts it to his own use: "He seems to create it anew for himself using what he hears as examples of language to learn from, not as samples of language to learn" (Cazden 1972, 91).

Given the reconstructive nature of language learning, then, it is not surprising that wordplay represents a regular accompaniment to the process. If, at these times, children focus on linguistic forms and functions, a case can certainly be made for the usefulness, if not necessity, of play to the language-learning process. It is in moments of play that youngsters are prompted to examine the makeup of the system through the violation of usual courses of communication. What follows are descriptions of common patterns of play found in the nursery classroom.

Conversation Conventions

Communication, it is unanimously agreed, is the major function of spoken or written language. Whether it is posing theories regarding the meaning of life or describing the beauty of a sunset, the basic intent of talk is to share thoughts, ideas, or feelings with another. Even when we engage in inner speech, we usually hypothesize a listener.

Learning to participate in social exchange is more than a matter of learning correct usage. It implies as well that the users understand the procedures and expectations guiding such exchanges. "Conversing," writes Garvey (1977, 72), "is a highly cooperative venture." Stated generally, speech events are understood as momentary alliances in which the participants can be trusted to speak the truth. Moreover, different types of exchange are governed by different conventions. Introductions of one person to another proceed through the use of highly formalized verbal phrases: "Mary, I'd like you to meet my friend John." In the past, such rules of decorum and guides for social exchange—what to say when—have been described in "politeness" books by people like Amy Vanderbilt and Emily Post. And while the carrying on of a conversation is done in a more spontaneous, haphazard fashion, expectations regarding how to proceed shift with changing topics; for example, different rules apply for the giving of directions than for the exchange of gossip.

At times, it is just these procedures and expectations—the conventions of conversation—that children delight in violating. Youngsters in the nursery years, for instance, having grasped the principle that conversational partners do not deliberately mislead one another, can often be heard to betray it. Witness the following exchange among two three-year-olds and their teacher in the schoolyard:

> *Simon:* [looking up the side of the school] What's way up there?
>
> *Teacher:* More classrooms.
>
> *Simon:* How do kids get up there?
>
> *Teacher:* What do you think?
>
> *Simon:* With a long, long ladder.
>
> [Max is listening to this exchange and grins at Simon's answer.]
>
> *Teacher:* What do you think, Max?
>
> *Max:* I think they got up there . . . [pauses and grins] in a cup!

Simon appears to be making a genuine effort to resolve the issue of how to get to the upper stories. Max, on the other hand, is apparently quite confident of how this is achieved and decides to suggest an outrageous possibility. He is teasing Simon.

Also typical of classroom question/answer frames are teachers' requests for information which they possess but which they want to make sure is also understood by their students. This differs from the more common question/answer frame used outside the classroom in which the questioner genuinely seeks information. In the above situation, Max seems to understand that the teacher knows the answer and further that he's expected to produce a "straight" response. In such cases, teachers can respond by enjoying one child's playfulness while making it clear to others who may be less well informed that this is a nonsensical proposition. In this situation, Simon indicates that he, like others (including Max), would benefit from trips to classrooms on the upper floors where he can see what goes on as well as look out the windows to the play yard below.

Children are, of course, expected to take teachers' (and most adults') assertions seriously. Moreover, they tend to be forbidden for the most part to express hostile or resentful feelings they might have toward their caretakers. In the context of play, though, children discover that subversive feelings can often be expressed without incurring reprisals (after all, play is play and not to be taken seriously). Such was the case in the following episode:

Daniel: [sitting with several other children peeling carrots] Wouldn't it be funny if these carrots were poison! [He laughs.] Wouldn't it be funny if there were no teachers! [He laughs harder.]

Molly: [sitting at the playdough table] I'm going to make a big cake . . . with lollipops over it . . . all colors . . . big ones.

Teacher: Molly, it sounds beautiful.

Molly: [with gusto] And they are all poison!

Daniel is considering the incongruous circumstances of "healthful" vegetables' having destructive elements and, even more outrageous, of teachers' being nonexistent. The last observation is a variation on the commonly debated theme in these years of what life would be like without adults. While it is often too threatening to consider life without parents (this comes later), teachers are potentially expendable.

Molly's sudden imbuing of lollipops with poison seems to spring from the impulse to refute or disagree with the teacher. She is momentarily distancing herself from this important adult in her life by offering a dissenting view. Such comments often represent a child's contemplation of the "independent" life and don't usually call for teacher comment. Fully aware of their dependence on adults, young-sters often experiment with taking initial steps toward independence by giving voice to differences of opinion.

A slightly different pattern of expectations for teacher/child exchange provides the impetus for three-year-old Ramsi's playful expression of resentment:

> Context: At the lunch table, a teacher begins a rather heavy-handed discussion of not talking with one's mouth full of food. She reiterates the sequence of what to do: take the food, chew it, swallow it, and then talk. She ends with this question: And after we swallow, then what can we do?
>
> *Ramsi:* [loudly and rapidly] We can dasha, we can basha, we can sasha, we can sash off, we can spit out!

A typical sequence of classroom exchange is: (1) teacher gives infor-mation, (2) teacher poses question that can be answered with the same information, and (3) children repeat the information. Ramsi vio-lates this sequence by responding with nonsense in lieu of the expected repetition of information. Such responses are typical of pre-schoolers when they feel unduly pressured into conforming responses. Their reactions clue teachers that either the form or the content of their messages, or both, need revising. While the use of this particular teaching sequence is sometimes appropriate, for the teaching of man-ners to a group of three-year-olds it is out of place, since most of them are incapable of consciously sequencing their actions in so precise a manner. And at lunch they are required to do two things at once—eat and be social. This is a feat in itself.

All teachers of nursery-age youngsters are familiar with another kind of violation of conversational conventions, namely the exploration of scatological material—"bathroom talk" as it is usually referred to—and its use in play. "Ca-ca," "doo-doo," "poo-poo," "doodie," etc., are names that children at times use for themselves, for peers, and, most often, for nothing, repeating them simply for the thrill of repetition—the last impulse motivated by the fact that repeating these words, even just for the fun of it, is taboo. These inevitable outbursts gener-ally represent nothing more than exuberant, but harmless, investi-gations of this taboo and usually don't require teacher comment.

The following episode describes a four-year-old's using "bathroom epithets" in an exchange with a friend (Rubin 1980, 55):

> Context: In the play yard, David and Josh are walking together and pretending to be robots.

> *David:* I'm a missile robot who can shoot missiles out of my fin-
> gers. I can shoot them out of everywhere—even out of
> my legs. I'm a missile robot.
>
> *Josh:* [tauntingly] No, you're a fart robot.
>
> *David:* [protestingly] No, I'm a missile robot.
>
> *Josh:* [recognizing that David is upset] And I'm a poo-poo
> robot.
>
> *David:* [in good spirits again] I'm a pee-pee robot.

By labeling David a "fart robot" Josh confounds his friend's expectations of the mutual cooperation and appreciation that accompanies
shared dramatic play. Such infractions, if continued, will usually ter-
minate the play sequence with one or more member leaving in tears or
anger. Josh, however, returns to the former friendly stance by producing a similar label for himself.

For children of nursery age, the exploiting of conversation conventions represents a constant element in the expanding modes of social
exchange. It is the violation of the convention that helps to clarify how
it should operate. Through playful but deliberate exploitations of
speech conventions children define and clarify for themselves accepted
boundaries of exchange.

Sense and Nonsense

Language, it is generally agreed, tries to describe reality. It is
designed, as the saying goes, to tell it like it is. Early on, this basic
tenet of language becomes the motivation for a kind of play involving
telling it like it *isn't*. Chukovsky ([1925] 1971, 97) describes his two-
year-old daughter's discovery of these possibilities for play:

> . . . somehow, one day, in the twenty-third month of her existence,
> my daughter came to me, looking mischievous and embarrassed at
> the same time—as if she were up to some intrigue. I had never
> before seen such a complex expression on her little face. She cried
> to me even when she was still at some distance from where I sat:
> "Daddy, 'oggie—meow!"—that is, she reported to me the sensa-
> tional and, to her, obviously incorrect news that a doggie, instead
> of barking, meows. And she burst out into somewhat encouraging,
> somewhat artificial laughter, inviting me, too, to laugh at this
> invention.
>
> But I was inclined to realism.
>
> "NO," said I, "the doggie bow-wows."

> "'Oggie—meow!" she repeated, laughing, and at the same time watched my facial expression which, she hoped, would show her how she should regard this erratic innovation which seemed to scare her a little.
>
> I decided to join in her game and said: "And the rooster meows!"

What Chukovsky gleaned from this and subsequent investigations of children's delight in nonsense was that such play holds a significant place in the child's cognitive development. Once the child is absolutely certain of the correct order of things, he writes, he or she delights in confirming this knowledge through the construction of its opposite. What his daughter realized was that "it was not dangerous to topsy-turvy the world according to one's whim, but on the contrary, it was even amusing to do so, provided that together with a false conception about reality there remained the correct one" (98).

Preschoolers I have taught are always sure to laugh at the part in Margaret Wise Brown's *Goodnight Moon* (1947) which has the reader bid "goodnight" to a brush and comb. Again, such descriptions defy the usual order of things, in this case treating inanimate objects as if they were animate. Language, these ages are finding, though usually in the service of representing things as they are, has the capacity to misrepresent as well. Indeed, in these explorations, youngsters are beginning to come to grips with a fundamental principle of word symbols—that they are arbitrary. While they can stand for things, they are not the things themselves. Hence they can be used to investigate and suggest ideas and actions beyond a straightforward representation of reality. With preschoolers, the absurdities words can describe are to be enjoyed for their own sake.

Children in the two-to-four age range reveal their grasp of what is sense and what nonsense through their responses to absurd descriptions of things. Nonsense play as a part of the linguistic repertoire tends to emerge during the third year. Garvey (1976, 40) recounts differences in the understanding of this kind of play revealed in an exchange between two-year-old Susie and her five-year-old brother David:

> Susie started to show me parts of her face, pointing to her eye, saying *eye*, then her nose, saying *nose*, and then her mouth. Her somewhat neglected brother[,] who had been watching, moved in and pointed to his forehead and said, quite dramatically, *Here's my mouth*. David and I laughed, then, but Susie was not amused.

David, who has long ago mastered this naming task, is exhibiting his competence by deliberately "misnaming" a part of his face. Susie, however, is still in the process of practicing a recently acquired skill and so is not yet ready to play in this way. Similarly, although many three-year-olds singing a song that invited them to rename the parts of Aiken Drum, an imaginary moon-dweller, could offer nonsensical substitutions for other parts of his body ("His legs," offered one girl, "are made out of . . . potatoes!"), Douglas, when asked to provide a substitute substance for "hair," thought for a while, and said very seriously, "Hair is made out of hair." Douglas was indicating that it was still necessary to confirm his developing understanding of how things are and was not yet ready to delight in misconstruing reality.

Chukovsky points out that traditional rhymes for these ages often exploit the child's love of nonsense by attributing the function of one object to another. Thus, he notes, it is true in both English and Russian verse that "seldom does anyone gallop on horseback, but more often on a cat or hen or some other unlikely animal" (90), e.g., "Tiny children / On tiny beetles / Went for a ride." The more farfetched the idea is, the better youngsters like it. These kinds of verses, dubbed by Chukovsky "topsie-turvies," deliberately construe an upside-down world.

The same group of three-year-olds that enjoyed "Aiken Drum" hit upon another way to play with absurdities generated by misnaming things. They created their own topsie-turvies by deliberately substituting names of things other than the tiger in the well-known "Eenie Meenie Minie Mo." A favorite version created by these New York City youngsters was:

> Eenie meenie minie mo
> Catch a subway by the toe
> If he hollers let him go
> Eenie meenie minie mo.

Sometimes the substitutions came from the domain of domestic animals; sometimes the children suggested their own names. And when we played the game at snack time, objects that were actually at hand— cups and crackers—were introduced. The latter substitutions, like "subway," were the most enjoyed, apparently because they were the most nonsensical. Children seem to enjoy such unequivocal misrepresentations of reality.

It is true that even in our era, some youngsters may have been exposed to the racist version of this verse in which "nigger" is substituted for "tiger." If this version is repeated in the classroom, it is likely to upset teachers more than children. At this age, such a rendition represents another form of name calling and should be treated as such— something "we don't do." I would caution teachers, at the same time, not to overdo their indignation, which can fuel rather than cure name-calling impulses. At later ages such social aberrations have more serious implications and require a broader response, as will be discussed in chapter 5.

Finally, teachers need to beware the tendency to suppress children's delight in absurdity by insisting upon literal or exact renditions of things. Such responses by adults are sometimes justified in that children's explorations of the absurd often occur at inopportune moments, but if such is the case amused tolerance and the recalling of the activity or focus on the agenda should permit things to proceed as planned. On the other hand, at regular and appropriate moments teachers can encourage nonsense play by appreciating children's inventions or construing nonsensical propositions themselves. During moments of chanting/repeating rhymes with one or two youngsters, I would sometimes say, "And dogs go meow and cats say bow-wow." Through their laughter, my listeners would invariably shriek, "No!" and then either correct me or join in the game, producing their own inversions. A book I often dipped into was Anno's illustrated collection of *Topsy-Turvies* (1970). While some of my group would try to "make sense" of the verses, many appreciated these expressions of the absurd. One of my colleagues, a teacher of four-year-olds who was keenly aware of her children's interest in conjuring up the absurd, began recording their descriptions, e.g., "The ant jumped over the Empire State Building." Eventually she put them in a book of "Nonsense Stories" with the children's illustrations. For a period, this book was the most popular one in the room. At each reading the youngsters laughingly and eagerly confirmed with each other and their teacher the silliness of their propositions. Eventually the teacher recognized the need for another book—about things that are "sensible" and can happen. In these ways, this group's renditions of "sense" and "nonsense" provided a lively context for exploring the possibilities of our language for representing—or *mis*-representing—how things are.

2 The Lilt of Language

Speculating about the origins of language, Suzanne Langer (1951) commented that humankind's penchant for constructing symbols representative of its experiences found a happy medium of expression in voice sounds. Not only are sounds in and of themselves especially arresting to our kind—"they annoy or please [us] even when they are not signs of anything further"—but they are also effortlessly produced by our voice mechanism (105). Through play with the vocal apparatus, we supply ourselves, Langer writes, "with interesting little phonetic items that can acquire conventional meanings because they carry no natural messages" (106). Indeed, it appears that so available and expressive an instrument as the human voice was (and is) well suited for capturing and communicating meanings shared by the members of our symbol-forming species.

Sheer delight in the musicality of voice sounds combined with word meanings is newly experienced by each succeeding generation of our young. Very soon after the infant begins smiling into the face of an adoring parent, he or she is regaled with rhythmic renditions of "Pat-a-cake, pat-a-cake, baker's man / Bake me a cake as fast as you can . . ." and other verses written for the very young. And while the toddler may run about half-singing, half-chanting partly remembered rhymes and songs, the more sophisticated preschooler is busy mastering a relatively extensive repertoire of traditional nursery rhymes repeated with parents, teachers, and peers. Indeed, as this and succeeding chapters testify, ways to play with the sounds of language are investigated throughout the three-to-eleven age range. In the preschool years, such activity serves two functions. It contributes to the child's phonological development, and it supports the poetic exploration of the sound resources of the language (Ferguson and Macken 1984). In the latter capacity, it represents an important thread in children's spontaneous exploration of the verbal arts. In this chapter describing preschoolers' play with sound, I first examine the relation of such play to the task of mastering speech sounds, and then describe how three-year-olds repeat and create language with a lilt in the classroom.

Categorizing Speech Sounds

In the beginning, the young language learner must sort the sounds of the system into identifiable groups. In his monograph investigating this process, Charles Read (1975) writes of this fundamental act of acquisition:

> Speech recognition itself is categorical. Without this property, speech communication as we know it would be impossible. If two discriminably different speech sounds could never be regarded as the same or functionally alike, we would recognize very few words, since almost all normal human utterances are noticeably different in some respect. (1)

This little-noted truth regarding the enormous variability of speech-sound reproduction points to the complexity of the task of acquisition. From exposure to the highly variable delivery of language sounds in speech events, children must derive the phonological categories representative of their native tongue. The task is made more difficult because spoken language is characterized by a continuous flow of word sounds. Yet it is out of this experience that youngsters organize the salient phonetic material constituting the phonological system of their language.

Aspects of pronunciation that help to set off or segment sequences of speech sounds are the prosodic features of stress, pitch, and pause. It is play with these, according to a study by Judith I. Schwartz (1977), which constitutes material for experimentation in infants of six to eighteen months and which could be described as "approximating American English pitch contour" (Schwartz 1981, 18). Then, too, the speech of the toddler is almost always delivered with attention to the expressive possibilities of sound (Anisfeld 1984; Ferguson and Macken 1984). Even in a one- or two-word utterance, two-year-olds can often be heard to move from highest to lowest points in their voice registers. Such attention to pitch often has the effect of making sound segments of the language more discernible than in normal adult speech.

In the same way, verse language—especially in children's rhymes—deliberately exploits prosodic characteristics of language:

> Humpty Dumpty sat on a wall
> Humpty Dumpty had a great fall
> All the king's horses and all the king's men
> Couldn't put Humpty together again.

This traditional favorite reveals the favorite form of children's verse—the four-beat couplet. In English, nearly all dandling rhymes, nursery rhymes, and game rhymes are constructed in this form, which quite naturally segments speech sounds, exposing and highlighting phonetic similarities and differences in a way that normal speech does not: HUMP-ty DUMP-ty SAT on a WALL / HUMP-ty DUMP-ty had a GREAT FALL . . . In their rhyme repetitions, young children tend to exaggerate the verse rhythms.

Nursery Rhymes in the Classroom

At the beginning of my year of teaching three-year-olds, I assumed that they, being born in the last quarter of the twentieth century, would no doubt find rhymes popular in eighteenth-century England unappealing. I was wrong. Within the first two weeks, I realized that in this school year, traditional rhymes could form the major source of our poetic play. I learned that most of them knew and could repeat with gusto "Jack and Jill," "Mary Had a Little Lamb," "Humpty Dumpty," and quite a few others. I saw, too, that repetition was the way it should be done. If we said them once, we said them dozens of times without any diminishing of enthusiasm. Also, and this was most important, I discovered that any attempts I might make to obscure rather than emphasize the repetitious (and, to me, tedious) sing-song cadences were not appreciated. The rhythm of the four-beat couplet, I found, might be exaggerated but never obscured.

Sound is the sensory aspect of speech. It is a tangible attribute of the symbol system that young children can manipulate to better acquaint themselves with that system's structures. In their rhyme repetitions, these three-year-olds were examining (and practicing) the sound patterns of their language. The force of the group's interest in traditional verses led me to end each morning with a group gathering called (appropriately) "Rhyme Time." In the course of the year, we developed an oral repertoire of thirty to forty favorite verses, including many songs.

After exploring traditional examples already a part of the group's repertoire, I began to search for other verses for us to learn. At Rhyme Time one morning I brought out a copy of *A Rocket in My Pocket* (Withers 1975), a collection of game chants and rhymes popular with slightly older children. I read the first selection:

> Way down South where bananas grow,
> A grasshopper stepped on an elephant's toe.
> The elephant said, with tears in his eyes,
> "Pick on somebody your own size."

When I had finished, the serious expression on everyone's face told me that the choice had not been a good one. Conceptually unable to appreciate the humor of the verse (this comes later), these three-year-olds appeared to identify with the plight of the elephant. I turned to other pages and read other, more appropriate, selections. At this point, I began to see that there were disadvantages to using a picture book at all. Unlike the repeating of rhymes from memory, these youngsters were now having to focus on pictures at the same time that they were being asked to concentrate on the verses. Though they would no doubt have gotten used to the pictures eventually, I decided that our Rhyme Time would be used for exploring verse sans books. Thus I needed to expand my memorized repertoire of verses in order to expand that of my three-year-olds.

In searching for material to bring to the group, I formed some criteria for what tended to be appropriate selections. Categories of verse popular with most preschoolers have one or more of the following characteristics:

1. Simple story line:

   There was a little turtle
   He lived in a box.
   He swam in a puddle
   He climbed on the rocks . . .

   ("The Little Turtle" by Vachel Lindsay)

2. Simple story line with finger play:

   There's such a tiny little mouse
   Living safely in my house
      [place forefinger in loosely clenched fist]
   Out at night he'll softly creep
      [creep fingers of one hand across the other]
   When everyone is fast asleep.
      [rest head on folded hands]
   But always in the light of day
      [spread hands and arms high and wide to represent sunrise]
   He'll softly, softly creep away.
      [creep fingers across hand again and whisk hand behind back]

3. Story in song with repeated chorus:

   "Old MacDonald's Farm"
   "The Mulberry Bush"

4. Verse/story with nonsense words:

   Hickory, dickory dock!
   The mouse ran up the clock.
   The clock struck one, the mouse ran down,
   Hickory, dickory dock!

5. Descriptions of daily actions:

> Slice, slice, the bread looks nice.
> Spread, spread the butter on the bread.
> On the top put jam so sweet.
> Now it's nice for us to eat.

6. Choral reading in which youngsters join in with rhymed words:

> I went downtown / To see Mrs. *Brown*.
> She gave me a nickel / To buy a *pickle*.
> The pickle was sour, / She gave me a *flower*.
> The flower was dead, / She gave me a *thread*.
> The thread was thin, / She gave me a *pin*.
> The pin was sharp, / She gave me a *harp* . . .

There are literally dozens of each type to be found in the many anthologies of children's verse. While three-year-olds can be counted upon to memorize verses four lines in length with relative ease, most have difficulty with longer rhymes. The group never tired, though, of hearing me repeat favorites like "Miss Polly's Dolly":

> Miss Polly had a dolly who was sick, sick, sick.
> She called for the doctor to come quick, quick, quick.
> The doctor came with his bag and his hat
> And he rapped on the door with a rat tat tat.
>
> He looked at the dolly and shook his head.
> And he said, "Miss Polly, put her straight to bed."
> He wrote on some paper for a pill, pill, pill.
> "I'll be back in the morning with the bill, bill, bill."

Only one or two would repeat parts of it with me. The teacher of the four-year-olds, on the other hand, described how many of her youngsters could repeat the entire poem, though some, like my three-year-olds, simply listened. A point to be stressed, then, is that listening—not only reciting—is an *active* effort for these ages as they focus on the musicality of their language.

Creating Language with a Lilt

Throughout the toddler and preschool years, children experiment spontaneously with language sounds. Sometimes youngsters explore the structure of a familiar word. One three-year-old was heard to break "yesterday" into syllables (yes/ ter/ day), mix up the syllables (yes/ter/yes/ter/day), put stress on different syllables (YES/ter/DAY), or simply repeat the syllables as a chant (Garvey 1977). Similarly, the snow falling outside our classroom prompted three-year-old Jonathan to pace the room chanting "SNOW snow, SNOW-Y snow-y, SNOW snow snow . . ." repeatedly. His words and actions gave eloquent expression to his eagerness to get outside.

Then, too, there is experimentation with onomatopoeia. In our culture children are particularly fond of repeating conventionalized sounds reputedly made by animals ("arf-arf," "meow," "baa," etc.) as well as action sounds for toy vehicles ("put-put," "beep," "varoom," etc.). Such sound representations of actions tend to accompany children's play throughout their elementary years. Youngsters simply shift sound structures to approximate the actions (rocket ship, explosions) they want to simulate.

The expressive use of word sounds also appears in many of my recordings of three-year-old students. In the middle of the school year, I began to record stories they were telling about their drawings and paintings. One morning, as Kimberly sat engrossed with crayons and paper, I invited her to tell me her story. She began: "Shama sheema / Mash day 'n' push day . . ." Though I expected a narrative, I realized (in time) that this poetic rendition of sounds was, indeed, a story worth recording. I wrote as she continued:

> 'N' mash day 'n' cash day
> 'N' mash day 'n' much day
> 'N' much day 'n' push day
> 'N' lush day 'n' push day.

At Rhyme Time, I read Kimberly's creation to the class. They listened with rapt attention. Someone asked that I "do it again." I did. At Rhyme Time the next day, Emily asked for "Kimberly's rhyme story." I read it many times during the next weeks and soon everybody began to say it with me. Subsequently, Nikki, among others, was prompted to produce a similar "story." This was also recorded and read to the class:

> Daz day 'n' daz day
> 'N' maz day 'n' maz day
> 'N' muz day 'n' laz day
> 'N' saz day.

Like Kimberly, Nikki was experimenting with substituting initial phonemes and repeating the same words in rhythmical sequence. A year later, Nikki, now four, greeted me after a long absence with "Hi, Linda . . . Binda, Minda Cinda." That this kind of play is a favorite one for these ages is not surprising when we consider that it uses the most popular rhyme form in children's traditional verses.

At another point in the year with this same group, I heard Kimberly singing/chanting a verse with the distinct rhythms of a popular song. I got my pad and pen and asked her to repeat it a little louder so I could write it down. Eyeing my pen and pad, she said *she* would write it down. I said I wasn't sure I could read her writing—so could she say it so I could write it and then she could write it her way? What I recorded was apparently her version of a rock song:

> Yes man, you say
> 'N' you wanna say
> You wanna say
> And run around
> Yes man, you wanna say
> And O K . . .
> Jumpety jumpety
> Jumpety jump
> And yuppy sup.

Taking my pad and pen in hand, Kimberly stopped singing and began to "write" her verse (fig. 1). Her writing is interesting because it reveals her view of recorded language. Indeed, her approximation of words-written-down has the "look" of manuscript. Like play with sound structures by themselves, this sample of early writing reveals this three-year-old exploring the form of recorded language separate from meaning.

Kimberly's and Nikki's selections provide evidence of the deliberate ordering and phrasing of the sound segments of their language. To ask youngsters to repeat or revise what has been produced would be to intrude fatally upon the process. The creations represent a blend of intuition, experimentation, and practice. With these ages, we have to get it the first time or not at all.

The rhymes were only part of an ever-increasing library of things children said that I recorded and read at group times, from which I have selected eight more examples. These accounts were produced spontaneously or in response to my request to tell about a drawing or an experience outside of school. Like the nonsense creations, these narratives are suffused with rhyme, rhythm, and repetition:

Judith and the Rain

> I love the rain coming down
> Because I love when it makes the drips
> They make too much music.

Liam and the Snow

> It's snow. We can't go outside.
> See the big pieces are falling.

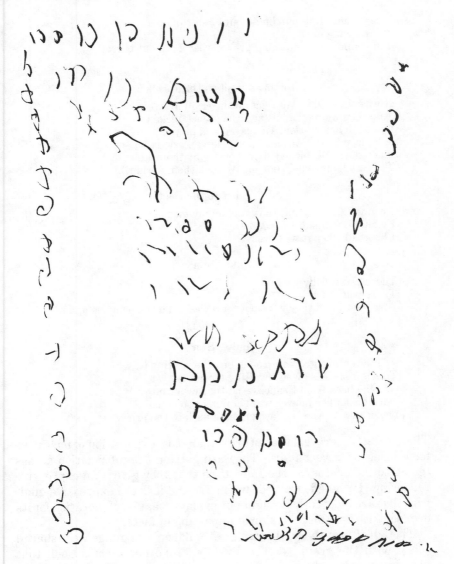

Figure 1. Kimberly writes her rhyme.

Ping! Bong! Pup pup bu bu bup! Peter popper.
It's snowing out!
I'm gonna taste those big pieces when I get out there!
Sure!

Tommy's Visit to Uncle Jack's

It was on Sunday. We went on the train first.
And then we took a bus and Uncle Jack picked us
up at the bus station. We played and played
and played. And we sleep and sleep and sleep for
many days. We picked strawberries by the field.
Then we had a whole bunch. We took them for lunch.

Edith's Visit to the Doctor

I whined when he put that stick in my mouth.
I whined, whined, whined.
I laughed when it was over.

Nikki's Story

There was a dolly wolly.
There was a house.
And then when they went out for a walk, they came home again.
'Cause it was too chilly.

Emily's Story

It's really a grown-up song but I'm writing it.
This is a princess who's waiting for her lawyer
to come back from France. And the lawyer never
came back. The lawyer was thinking about the
princess . . . And the lawyer came back to the princess.

These selections reveal these three-year-olds' exploration of narrative form along with verbal art. They are getting the information across (going to the doctor) at the same time that they give it an expressive rendering (I whined, whined, whined). And it is the expressive qualities that are most fully brought out in play—that is, elaboration for its own sake rather than the simple imparting of facts.

Though at first these recordings of children's language were shared solely with the group, eventually I put together a class book that included a sample from each child and made a copy for each to take home. I also made copies of our rhyme repertoire for my students' parents and encouraged them to repeat them with their youngsters. It is especially important to involve parents in the appreciation of children's love of rhyme as well as their efforts at creating stories, since such rhyming is often merely tolerated rather than encouraged by the preschooler's parents. Teachers can educate these key people in youngsters' lives not only through what they express directly about children or the program but also through what they choose to record and share of children's productions.

The Transition Years
(Five through Seven)

3 The Art of Nonsense

Like preschoolers, children in the primary grades (five through seven years old) delight in verbal nonsense. "I saw Superman flying out there," quipped five-year-old Josh in response to his teacher's request for descriptions of what had been observed on a class walk around the block. After Josh's opener, one nonsensical description followed another as the children happily explored the potential of language for conjuring up the absurd.

In recent decades, these ages have come to be known as the transition years. For the most part, this label is meant to describe the intellectual transformation children experience during this time. As Piaget and Inhelder (1969) have defined it, during this period youngsters shift from preoperational views of things to concrete operational thinking. Thus the preschooler's reliance on perceptual variables as a major source of understanding—airplanes appear smaller in the air than on the ground, so they must shrink—is expanded to include logical structures for reasoning about how things work—"shrinking" airplanes can be explained by the influence of distance upon the perception of size. As documented by Piaget and many others, this shift in intellectual perspectives occurs gradually during the early childhood years, and its so-called completion cannot be correlated with a specific chronological age. Most children, however, achieve the later stage of development by eight years of age. A heterogeneous grouping of six-year-olds, then, would include youngsters at varying levels of intellectual maturity. Educators of the primary grades often find that such differences in development translate into a greater or lesser ability to comprehend how symbols (numerals and written language, for the most part) operate. In fact, in many classrooms these differences alone define who's "getting it" and who isn't, since most teaching/learning strategies in the primary grades—especially those represented in commercial programs—assume that youngsters can handle concepts and abstractions appropriate for later stages of comprehension. The early childhood educator, more than any other, is called upon to understand a wide range of intellectual behaviors and to provide appropriate programs for children who fall at different points on the developmental continuum. As Eleanor Duckworth (1979) puts it, the process of teaching these ages is largely a matter of understanding where the learner is in his or her understanding. The teacher who is unable to share the child's view of things and to use this information to develop instructional strategies considerably undermines his or her educational impact. Interestingly, children often reveal where they are in their growth through their grasp of particular aspects of wordplay. It is this developmental perspective on stages of wordplay that I will examine next.

Nonsense—Pure and Logical

The following joke was told by six-year-old David to his teacher:

> You wanna hear a joke? Well, see, there were these two carrots driving down the road and their car had a crash and they both had to go to the hospital . . . see . . . and one of them was okay, see, an' went home and then he called back to find out how the other carrot was and the doctor said . . . "Well, I have good news and bad news. The good news is that he's gonna live, but the bad news is that he'll be a carrot all his life!" . . . Get it?

At this point David, after having been suffused with giggles throughout the telling, became convulsed with laughter. Quite unaware that the punch line should have been ". . . he'll be a vegetable all his life"—being a carrot was an acceptable as well as comprehensible substitute—David found the joke thoroughly delightful.

In its design, the joke mixes two types of humor—what Paul McGhee (1972) has called *pure incongruity* and *logical incongruity*. Descriptions of carrots that can talk, drive cars, etc., is pure nonsense; they provide the context for the punch line. The humor of the joke is derived from the use of "vegetable" as a pun and the juxtaposing of the literal and figurative meanings of this word. This strategy is a type of logical incongruity. Both teller and listener are delighted by the construction of a narrative that ends in the projection of two meanings for a single word or phrase.

David's delight, however, is with the purely nonsensical part of the joke. Carrots endowed with human qualities are what he finds incongruous. For him, like many others his age, images of a nonsensical world appear to be played out in his mind's eye as he repeats the joke. It is during the next age/stage of humor comprehension—the middle elementary years—that play with logical incongruities becomes part of youngsters' repertoire of joke strategies. Unlike David, the more sophisticated eight- to eleven-year-old more or less gets over the nonsense to get to the joke. And though delight in nonsense continues as a part of the later-elementary and adult strategies of humor, its greatest champions tend to be youngsters in the five-to-seven age range, who, along with their preschool allies, endlessly explore the possibilities of turning the world topsy-turvy through their appreciation and creation of nonsensical descriptions of things.

Learning to tell a joke is in itself a complex task. In the carrot joke, David grapples, successfully, with a relatively complex text structure. It takes some story-telling skill to organize the material so that the context for the punch line is properly set up. Indeed, mastery of joke rhetoric, like mastery of the structures of riddles, rhymes, and tongue twisters, poses some problems for our five- to seven-year-olds. Like David, though, most willingly wrestle with these difficulties as they explore and expand their wordplay repertoires. Finally, the creations of these ages, though often exemplary of nonsensical humor, also represent explorations of logical incongruities or "true" joke strategies. Thus in the samples included below, we see many youngsters beginning to come to grips with the occurrence (frequent in our language) of words and phrases with more than one meaning.

Riddle Rhetoric

"Why are fish so smart?" proposes the artful riddler to the riddlees. When no answer is forthcoming, the triumphant questioner crows, "Because they go around in schools!" The riddle paradox, as it has come to be known, often derives its surprise from a play on words. In this example the two different meanings of "school" are playfully explored as if they were one. Though children in the transition years are among the staunchest supporters of riddle play, most are still in the throes of sorting out the many elusive elements of this form. Most, like David, are not yet able to detect—much less play with—ideas such as the multiple meanings of the "school." However, that doesn't stop these ages from participating in a group riddling session. (It doesn't stop them from laughing, either, even though they don't really "get it.")

What Is a Riddle?

At these ages, children are initially occupied with understanding the particular format of question and answer. Often a child produces what she or he regards as a riddle question—"Why is the sky?" Subsequently, the child disavows suggested answers and is dumbfounded when asked, finally, to reveal the solution by the expectant audience. The child believes that the question alone is the whole riddle.

At other times, question and answer are supplied but a connection between the two is missing: "Why was the whale eating the shark?" (Because he wanted to get in a taxi). What is expressed in this example is the child's interpretation of riddle paradox as simple capriciousness (Sutton-Smith 1976).

Unable yet to exploit anomalies, either linguistic or conceptual, children direct the bulk of their efforts at this stage toward organizing some sort of "fit" between question and solution. Often, the connection between question and answer is derived from motivation: "Why did the farmer pull off his coat when he went into the water?" (Those were his best clothes) (McDowell 1979, 201). Expressions of causality frequently appear in the productions of these riddlers: "Why was a shark eating a boat?" (Because it was a fishing boat and he wanted to eat the fish). In the same mode are those efforts that enumerate object properties: (1) "What's red?" (A rose) (McDowell 1979, 35); and (2) "What has five sides and lives in the sea?" (A starfish) (McDowell 1979, 35). In the latter examples, the child is examining the role of language in describing the stuff of the world through a cataloging of objects and their attributes. John McDowell (1979) labels these productions "descriptive" riddles.

Five-Year-Old Riddlers

Early in the school year, a kindergarten teacher reported to me, a spontaneous riddling session began at the snack table. At this point no formal introduction to riddles had taken place. As the children produced riddles, the teacher recorded them. In the next few days the teacher took steps to prepare this collection of fifteen riddles for representation in a class book. Each offering was printed on a separate page with space for a picture. These selections were read back to the children, who were as delighted by hearing their creations as they had been when producing them. Pictures were drawn to accompany the riddles, the pages were clipped together, and a cover with a title was made. The book was placed in the class library and was "read" again and again by small groups or individuals. Subsequent riddle sessions were held—most often initiated by the children—and their creations recorded and added to this collection.

In the initial group of fifteen, only one selection could be considererd a true riddle: "Why did the elephant put crayons in his bed?" (Because he wanted to have colorful dreams). Obviously, the child was repeating something previously heard. Traditionally, in fact, this example is found in the corpus of "moron" riddles. In the repetition of the riddle, this five-year-old substituted "elephant"—adding the element of non-sense—for "moron," the meaning of which is probably not understood. Standard strategy at this stage is to incorporate nonsense whenever understanding is missing. Yet the repetition of a true riddle by a five-year-old indicates an advanced understanding of riddle humor. (It also alerts us to the necessity of relying more on stage than on age for determining a child's level of riddling competence.) Most children in this age/stage, however, cannot remember, much less reproduce, riddles whose paradoxes elude them. In this particular example, the deception derives from the suggestion of a literal interpretation for the figuratively employed adjective "colorful."

All of these riddlers provided both question and answer and, as the following samples indicate, their efforts can be classified as either descriptive or nonsensical or both: (1) "Why did the alligator put on his baseball clothes?" (Because he was going to the alligator baseball place); (2) "Why did the turtle go out of his shell?" (Because he was getting too big for it); (3) "Why did the cat want to catch a snake?" (Because he wanted to turn into a rattlecat). The producer of "rattle-cat" is already beginning to grasp the nature of riddle humor as deriv-ing, at times, from manipulations of word meanings. These kinds of productions characterize the riddle play of the early elementary years and, although these efforts may seem foolish to adults, they are as delightful (and instructive) to these youngsters as the producing of true riddles is subsequently (fig. 2).

Soliciting Descriptive Riddles

In addition to appreciating early riddle efforts teachers will want to encourage these ages to create descriptive riddles:

1. What is thin and round and has a point at one end? (Pencils, cra-yons, magic markers, nails, etc.)
2. What can cut things? (Scissors, knives, saws, etc.)

In the formulation of descriptive riddles, children explore methods of describing the stuff of their world. The riddle question enumerates attributes of the item(s) named in the answer. The above examples are meant to be posed in the classroom. Group riddling sessions can easily be structured to invite children to invent their own examples. Prompt-ing children to draw on items in the classroom means that their pro-ductions derive from an immediately visible as well as common frame of reference for all members of the group. When appropriate, other

Why was the whale eating the shark?

because he wanted to get in a taxi.

Why did the alligator put on his baseball clothes?

because he was going to the alligator baseball place.

Figure 2. Two riddles by five-year-olds

areas or categories of items can be added (things in the playground, in the lunchroom, at the seashore). In describing areas or items of experience which, for the moment, are out of sight, children have the opportunity to exercise powers of memory and definition different from those required for the description of objects then visible.

In recording their inventions, children should be encouraged to write the question on one side of the paper and the answer on the other. Then when the riddles are clipped together in book form, the reader has the chance to deliberate possible answers before encountering those supplied by the inventor.

The discussions stimulated by the exploration of descriptive riddles are especially significant to the development of defining and classifying skills. Children should be given the opportunity to articulate general characteristics of these riddles: the question describes the thing(s) in the answer, i.e., what it looks like and/or what it does. In formulating these aspects of descriptive riddles children begin to derive key patterns of word definitions:

> The meanings of word-names derive from the *appearance* of the items as in 1 above.

> The meanings of word-names derive from the *functions* of the items as in 2 above.

During the elementary years, as noted, youngsters are called upon to define familiar words, to make up sentences indicating the meanings of words, and to consciously extend their vocabularies through the differentiation of attributes of new and old words. In working through these tasks, children will benefit from opportunities to explore—through descriptive riddling—key features from which word meanings derive, i.e., appearances and functions.

Sound, Sense, and Symbol

"A rose," Shakespeare writes, "by any other name would smell as sweet . . ." In this phrase, the playwright, with characteristic economy, describes the nature of words. They are not things; they stand for things. There is no intrinsic connection between a name and its referent—the relation is purely arbitrary. This fact of verbal symbols appears to penetrate the child's understanding around school age. Previously, word-names tended to be understood as intrinsic attributes of the objects/experiences they describe—indeed, they appear to come and go, with the comings and goings of things and events

(Brown 1973). Children's subsequent separation of "word" and "thing" points to their developing sense of the abstractness of the language system. In their play with word sounds and sense, children often provide clues to the way they acquire an understanding of the symbolic nature of words.

Homophones

What contributes to an emerging sense of word-as-symbol is the discovery that many words sound the same but have different meanings. Children's sensitivity to word sounds allows them, more often than adults, to "hear through" context and to connect words with different meanings by their sound identities. Witness six-year-old Sarah's discoveries about teachers' names, told to me and her friend Gwynne on a walk through our school:

> Sarah: And Ms. Stone is a stone. Ms. Crowe is a crow. [She flaps her arms.] Ms. Leaf is a leaf. And Ms. Suller is a big basement! [She laughs.]

> Gwynne: Her name is *Sull*-er, not cellar! [We pass by the three-year-olds' room and nod to Ms. Seigel.]

> Sarah: And Ms. Seigel is a sea gull!

Children's discoveries may be representative of homophony (like Sarah's) or polysemy (words with metaphorically related meanings— "schools" of fish and education). It doesn't matter. To the five- or six-year-old what is striking is that a single sound sequence describes separate domains of experience. These discoveries provide evidence that conflicts with the idea that word-names and their referents might be intrinsically related. The logical extension of that premise is that different things would be described by different (word) sounds. This is not always the case, children discover, as they confront instances of the anomalous same-sound/different-meaning pattern. Just as the bilingual child's separation of word and thing is enhanced by knowing two names for a single item (Leopold 1970), so the English-speaking child's understanding of word-as-symbol appears to be aided by the frequent occurrence of homophonic and polysemous structures of words/phrases in our language.

With a certain inevitability, our five- and six-year-olds "discover" particular categories of words—Sarah's proper name/common name being one—derivative of the same-sound/different-meaning structure:

1. Words with different roots or derivations, e.g., *sun/son; red/ read; pair/pare/pear*

2. Sound identities between letter or number names/words, e.g., *b/ to be/bee; ate/eight*
3. Sound identities created through the shifting of word boundaries, e.g., *Seigel/sea gull; lettuce/let us*
4. Polysemy, e.g., *run* (to move quickly)/*run* (to flow as in running water)

Picking up on and exploiting children's discovery of examples of this pattern can be a regular part of the kindergarten and first- and second-grade programs. Such discoveries can be gathered on an experience chart: "We discovered that some words sound the same but have different meanings." The discoverer can prepare a pictorial lexicon to accompany the discovery (fig. 3). Susan's pictorial definition of "hair" and "hare" was part of a class book in which other such discoveries were similarly presented. In preparing these discoveries thus, children become involved in clarifying and defining sound/meaning relations of these word pairs.

Figure 3. Homophone

A teacher of a combined class of six- and seven-year-olds stimulated exploration of this pattern by starting a class discussion with the sentence "Jim is in the gym." The children were intrigued by this frame for exploring these sound/meaning relations and, after examining another example, began producing their own. Here are three from the twenty they invented:

> Nobody knows what's in your nose.
>
> I had a ball bouncing a ball.
>
> There's a hole in my whole wholewheat bread.

The teacher recorded these often nonsensical sentences as they were produced and subsequently transcribed them as a class book.

End Rhymes

Nonsensical rhyme play can be initiated through the reading of Walter Einsel's (1962) delightful *Did You Ever See?* The book is a sequence of silly questions—"Did you ever see a crow . . . row?"—with appropriately absurd illustrations. Subsequently children can be invited to create their own nonsensical descriptions in words and pictures. In addition to the examples in figure 4, a group of kindergartners produced these "did you ever see" captions (with pictures) for a class book:

> Did you ever see a tomato in a tornado?
>
> Did you ever see a book cook?
>
> Did you ever see a car hang on a bar?

Observing youngsters create such nonsense, one feels a lingering sense of word magic. It comes through in the ease and vividness with which they record the absurd imagery suggested by the phrases. Like poets, children seem to see what they say.

Alliteration

A strategy for creating tongue-twisters favored by the primary ages is the use of alliteration. The same group of six- and seven-year-olds who produced the homophone sentences composed a story about "The Sleepy Old Sailboat and the Shy Old Sailor":

> Slowly the sleepy old sailboat sailed through the salty sea. The skipper was a shy old sailor. So were the other sailors. But they sailed on. Suddenly a shark and so many salamanders started sawing through the ship. So did a nearby swordfish. So they abandoned the ship and swam for shore. But what happened to the

Figure 4. "Did you ever see keys with knees?"

sailors? One sailor made it to shore. He was the shyest of the sixty-seven sailors. All the rest of the sailors were so scared. They let some of the sharks, salamanders, and swordfish swallow them. Some of their names were Sammy Sambrick the Stealer, Sylvester Sicklebore, Sally the Sailor, Stacha, Satan, Sara, Susie Stoogehead, and Samberdee.

This class effort was subsequently recorded and copies were run off for every child.

For these ages, writing a story according to a certain rhetorical frame is best undertaken as a group. What can be an overwhelming task for one child is easily mastered when many minds can be used as resources.

These ages, however, are quite capable of creating tongue-twisters using the alliteration frame. They might be helped by following this sequence of steps:

1. Choose a word that names an animal/object/place—bear, for instance.

2. Identify the sound of the initial phoneme—/b/.

3. Think of other words that begin with the same or similar sound and which may describe this thing—

big	barking	basin
black	bathing	bottom
brown	burping	. . .

4. Play with different possibilities for making up a tongue-twister with these words—

> Big Burping Bears
> Black Bears Bark

5. Choose one or more to record in words and pictures.

In creating tongue twisters, children can be encouraged to note differences and similarities in patterns of alliteration. Finally, they can be helped to articulate the general patterning of alliteration: the beginnings of words in the phrase have the same or similar sounds but the ending sounds are different.

Onomatopoeia

As noted, word symbols are arbitrary. "Cats" could just as well be called "dogs" or vice versa and nothing about either animal would be affected. Names simply represent reality—they are not things in themselves. There is, though, one category of words that defies this general definition. With great delight, young children match objects/actions and their sounds ("meow," "ding-a-ling") and consider these onomatopoeic constructions some of the most interesting in their growing vocabularies. In the nursery classroom, these inventions are often found in books and songs. In "Old MacDonald's Farm," for example, the animals that inhabit the farm are identified by name ("pig") and noise ("oink-oink").

In the primary years, youngsters are fascinated by the sheer aural expressiveness generated by words in this category. And, often, incongruous uses for these constructions are enjoyed, as in this poem by Spike Milligan (in Cole, 1969):

> A thousand hairy savages
> Sitting down to lunch
> Gobble gobble glup glup
> Munch munch munch.

In the early elementary years, children can be invited to explore words whose sounds suggest their meaning. A teacher might focus children's attention on this idea by asking:

What words might you use to describe the sounds of . . .

opening a can of soda

noisy eating

pebbles being dropped in a puddle

china plates falling on the floor?

Certain images and actions will be more fruitful than others in eliciting words with distinct onomatopoeic characteristics. In choosing images to stimulate children's thinking, teachers need to consider familiar and/or meaningful areas for a group to explore. City children, for example, will respond to different possibilities and may have words in their vocabularies not available to youngsters who live in the country, and vice versa.

Teachers may want to record children's discoveries on a chart headed "Sometimes the sounds of words can express their meaning . . ." Or, for this task, as with most of the wordplay tasks for these ages, children can be encouraged to record their discoveries in words ("pop," "hiss," "fizz") and pictures (an open can of soda).

Some Final Words

For the primary years, then, nonsense play represents a specific method for exploring the nature of the language system. Conceptually, as noted earlier, youngsters are often engaged in the process of confirming how things work by exploring how they don't. In language play, this frequently means describing a world that doesn't exist—telling it like it isn't—as a way of exhibiting mastery over what *is*.

Simultaneously, children explore the poetic resources of the language in their play. Patterns in sound represented by intonation, rhyme, and rhythm are carefully examined in spontaneous play, as well as in the ritual repetitions of traditional play forms. Whereas Lewis Carroll's advice was to "take care of the sense and the sounds will take care of themselves," to some extent these ages do the opposite: they take care of the sounds and let the sense, at times, be nonsense.

In addition, children are beginning to master rhetorical patterns found in jokes, riddles, and verse. Exploration of these forms of sound, sense, and text—forms similar to those found in adult expressions of eloquence—suggests that children's speech play is instrumental to the acquisition of adult verbal art. It is, write Sanches and Kirshenblatt-Gimblett (1976), as though children are in the process of "acquiring the poetry of grammar as preparation for the acquisition of the grammar of poetry" (106). In the succeeding stage of development, the eight-to-eleven age range, these same aspects of verbal art are explored in speech play forms. In the middle elementary years, however, children's repertoire of play tends to grow in its diversity, in the competence of its execution, and in the complexity of its exploitation of patterns of sound, sense, and rhetoric.

As we move beyond the nursery years, and closer to a curriculum in which teachers are shapers and designers of students' daily activities, it is important to remember that wordplay, like all language education programming, must be explored in context. Youngsters should not suddenly be asked to produce riddles or rhymes on the assumption that, because they like to repeat them, these are forms of which they can easily create examples. Only a few can do that—those youngsters we've all met who pick things up quickly and who seem to be their own best teachers. Nor should children be asked to study the "elements" of the form (workbook style) as a way of understanding how to create within a particular genre. At this age such a method tends to undermine the impulse to play, wrongly assuming that descriptions of rules for rhyme or meter will enhance "poetic" intuitions. In fact, such a process is a method only appropriate for the adult learner, who, presumably, has been amply exposed to examples of a particular form over a long period of time.

In the primary years, teachers must first build in regular exposure to wordplay forms through the reading of books, the scheduling of group exchanges of favorite rhymes and riddles, and/or by having the group do some chanting of popular rhymes in unison. Sooner or later, some children will spontaneously begin to create their own versions. These can be recorded and "played back" to the group, since teacher interest in such creations tends to stimulate other children to try out these possibilities. As children's creations are collected in class books, it often takes little more to keep a wordplay program alive than reminding students during the reading/writing time that they may want to add to the "Did you ever see . . ." book or the riddle anthology, or to record yet another favorite in the class book of chants. The point to be stressed is that once the teacher provides a regular place in the program for exposure to these forms, children are more likely to show an interest in pursuing one aspect or another of wordplay. When students begin to produce their own creations, teachers need only be alert to where they seem to be heading and to provide time, materials, and guidance as needed to help them record, expand, and share their productions.

4 Reading, Writing, and Rhyming

Day by day, five-, six-, and seven-year-olds continue the oral tradition of game chants and rhymes. These are years when youngsters constantly practice and compete in their abilities to snap fingers, whistle, throw and catch a ball, and jump rope. Nearly identical in form to the once-loved nursery rhymes, game chants guide the flow of movement. They indicate "who's in" and "who's out" and when to perform a clap or jump. Intent upon the actions guided by the verses, children make necessary adjustments by speeding up or slowing down their repetition of the verse and by eliminating irregularities in syllable structures that might disrupt the rhythm.

The verses can be categorized according to the functions they perform. There are counting-out rhymes: "Acka backa soda cracker / Acka backa boo / Acka backa soda cracker / Out goes you." There are rope-skipping chants: "Last night and the night before / Twenty-four robbers came to my door / When I went down to let them in / They knocked me down with a rolling pin / Ten ran east and ten ran west / And four jumped over the cuckoo's nest" (player jumps out) (Emrich 1970). And, of course, ball-bouncing rhymes: "1-2-3-O'Leary / 4-5-6-O'Leary / 7-8-9-O'Leary / 10-O'Leary—Postman!" And, finally, there are the not-to-be-forgotten teases and taunts, a familiar part of the "social" exchange of these years: "Roses are red / violets are blue / If I looked like you / I'd join the zoo." Though adults are purveyors of nursery rhymes to one preschool generation after another, children from six to eleven are the protectors and transmitters of their own extensive tradition of verbal art. Together they ensure the perpetuation of a body of material expressive of humankind's love of words in verse.

Spontaneous chanting, a frequent accompaniment to the play of three-year-olds, continues into these years. School-age chanters often explore syllable shapes and the sounds of proper names (Opie and Opie 1959). A typical example, discovered by nearly every group in which there is a girl named "Anna," is play with variations on this sound pattern: "fanna," "sanna," "manna," etc. Inevitably this exploration produces "banana." "Anna banana," once discovered, will be repeated to tease, of course, but also because of a delight in the similarities in sound of words with very different meanings. Here, children play with the notion that sound similarities between words just might indicate similarities in meaning. "Anna," the playful supposition goes, just might have something in common with "banana."

Also during these years a significant change in youngsters' educational lives takes place. In our culture the primary years are those in which youngsters begin their formal education. It is during their sixth year that children are required to become members of first-grade groups. For most youngsters this is an introduction to what will become the most important social community outside their homes for the next twelve years.

Undoubtedly, the main emphasis in the early grades is on literacy learning. For most of this century, it has been well understood that in order to participate successfully in the economic, political, and cultural arenas, one must be a competent reader. Hence, the early focus is on learning to read so that in subsequent years students can turn to reading to learn. In the last decade, there has been a move to "balance the basics," as Donald Graves (1978) has put it, and to provide equal time for the development of youngsters' writing/composing abilities. Then, too, recent research on speaking and literacy learning has begun to document relations between the two. In the main, researchers are making it clearer and clearer that developments in oral and written language abilities are more alike than different and that they are largely self-regulatory in nature (Brown 1973; Holdaway 1979; Smith 1979). Through exposure to language in use—spoken and written—children reconstruct for themselves the rules of the system. Further, these researchers and others propose that educators engaged in guiding the development of children's language abilities need to take a "whole language approach" (Holdaway 1984) and design programs that provide ample exposure to, and opportunities for, speaking, reading, and writing. In constructing environments for language learning, especially for the primary ages, educators need to consider how useful a source children's traditional verses are in helping youngsters understand the nature of print.

Predictable Text and Beginning Reading

In an address to the 1982 International Reading Association Conference, Kenneth Goodman summarized his view of beginning stages of literacy learning: "Reading begins with whole meaningful texts which are easily predictable for the learners." "Predictable" is the key word. In Goodman's terms, it points to the need to match meanings expressed in print with those that are already a part of the child's developing grasp of language forms and functions. Children's verse is one example. It is "whole" in the sense of having a content expressible in four to six lines; it is "meaningful" in that it is familiar and enjoyable to children; and it is "predictable," of course, because verse language, by definition, is characterized by sound patterning.

Given recordings of their own rhymes and chants, children can read the material before they can identify words in or out of context. They simply let their memories do the work. Many teachers of reading have suffered from the erroneous notion that such experiences do not represent "real" reading, an activity they narrowly define as the decoding of material never before encountered—whether orally, by speaking their own creations, aurally, by hearing others give theirs, or visually. Beginning readers need help into the world of print and can learn a great deal about recorded language through opportunities to make connections between oral language and its representation in print. Subsequent encounters with familiar material can then include work on developing sight vocabulary. The introduction as well of verses not yet part of the child's memory bank contributes other supports to the beginner. The use of rhyme is not only satisfying to the ear—and much early reading is done aloud—but also aids the reader by limiting the choice of words, allowing young readers to make use of the predictability of verse language. They have long understood, with their ears if not their intellects, that words in verse rhyme with those before or after. This plus the contextual clues provided by rhythm are useful tools for deciphering print, and repetition of the same words (a hallmark of most basal readers) is quite naturally represented in many of children's favorite verses.

Finally, it should be noted that intonation patterns important to the comprehension of any text (Pearson and Fielding 1982) are only very inadequately transcribed in English, since punctuation provides only limited assistance regarding stress and pitch patterns. Many beginning readers, in fact, are permitted to intone their way through unfamiliar material with little or no expression, and in fact they usually have no alternative, since it is difficult to give an appropriate rendering of the sounds until one understands the sense. Because verse language is constructed upon a predictable and familiar sound pattern, on the other hand, beginning readers can make use of this knowledge to help them read rhymes with sense and fluency.

Developing programs for getting into reading through the use of children's verses might begin, when appropriate, with four-year-olds. The same teacher who constructed the "sense/nonsense" book, for example, decided to exploit her very successful program of rhyme repetition by recording three favorites in a class book. Each verse of four lines was printed in large letters in a different color, in dry-mark pen, one line to a page. Pictures accompanied the text. The book was an immediate hit and was read daily for a time. The reading often turned into a group repetition of the verses as the teacher turned the pages. Before long, some youngsters would pick up the book and say the rhymes as they flipped through the pages—not bothering to match their oral repetition with the print. Afterward, however, they often announced, proudly, that they had read the book. Slowly, some of these same children began to connect the right verse with the right color print. And, finally, some moved on to reading/repeating the verse line for line, pointing to the words—correctly. This kind of experience can contribute much to the beginner's familiarity with print forms. A basic understanding with which beginners grapple is the concept of the word. Speech, we know, does not provide children with definitive boundaries for separating one sound/meaning conglomerate from another. The "reading" of memorized verse can contribute to the child's developing grasp of the concept of discrete words and their meanings (Morris 1981).

Another way to capitalize upon young children's affinity for rhyme play is revealed by a group of kindergartners and their teacher. At snack time one morning, a catchy couplet was being bandied about: "Monkey, monkey, sitting in a tree / Monkey, monkey, can't catch me." Very likely it was a truncated version of a teasing verse one of the children had heard some older youngsters repeat. After a few repetitions, one child came up with a new version: "Monkey, monkey, sitting in a tree / Monkey, monkey, fall off me." This play with the final phrase was picked up by others and soon the last line had four additional endings: "go to three"; "count to three"; "boom boom bee"; and "with a bee." The teacher recorded each new version and the original couplet on a separate sheet of paper and the creators supplied pictures. These sheets were clipped together to form a class book which was placed among the group's reading materials.

As children's repertoire of traditional game chants expands, the new as well as the old can be recorded as a class anthology or mimeographed so that each child can build his or her own collection. Some groups of first and second graders will be ready to explore the history of these verses by asking adult members of their families about rhymes and chants with accompanying games popular in "the olden days." The discovery that many of their verses were once part of parents' and grandparents' lives—indeed, often in identical forms—comes as a shock to children of these ages. Such surprises make a good beginning to a social studies program by focusing children's attention on their personal "roots" and on the stability and longevity of their oral tradition.

The suggestion, then, is not that an entire beginning reading program be developed solely around the reading of verse language. As Frank Smith (1977) reminds us, print is different from speech: "Spoken language has adapted itself to being heard while written language is more appropriately read" (391). Children need to become acquainted with certain basic distinctions between speech and print through exposure to a variety of forms and functions of each. Interestingly, though, Smith's description of differences between spoken and written language is true for almost all verbal creations *except* those that attempt to enhance their meaning through the exploitation of verbal art. Verse language—whether adult or children's poetry, lyrics, traditional rhymes, etc.—is designed to be said as well as read. And though perhaps inspired by possibilities of oral performance, such verbal creations may nonetheless be preserved in print so that they can be easily retrieved and shared with others distant in time and space—hence their efficacy as material for reading/reciting. Further, as Smith points out, beginning steps in reading acquisition involve a coming to grips with such key metalinguistic terms as "sentence," "paragraph," the already mentioned "word," etc., an understanding best acquired in the act of reading. And because the reading/repeating of familiar verses relieves the beginner of some of the task of discovering *what* is being said, it can leave him or her freer to consider *how* it is being said—how, that is, spoken language is represented by print systems.

Learning to Spell

In the last decade, research has defined a developmental course in learning to spell (Bissex 1980; Chomsky 1979; Henderson and Beers 1980; Read 1975). Beginners invited to invent their own spellings tend to rely upon phonetic strategies for transcribing word sounds into print. Their writing reflects a systematic though nonstandard use of letter names and/or sounds for representing words: "R U DF?" (Are you deaf?) (Chomsky 1979). "What is interesting," writes Chomsky, "is that different children invent very much the same system of spelling"

(44). Moreover, children find a way to resolve the fact that the English alphabet does not provide enough symbols to represent its over forty sound units. They readily double up in their use of letters, indicating an ability to deal with organizing principles more abstract than that exemplified by a one-to-one, sound-to-spelling match. As they move toward conventional spelling, children must, in fact, come to grips with three main sources (or "rules") of orthographic variability: (1) The same sound can be represented by different spellings, e.g., the long *e* in "see," "receive," etc.; (2) different sounds can be represented by the same spelling, e.g., the letter *y* in "yes," "gym," etc.; and (3) letters can combine to stand for a unique sound, e.g., *sh* in "shoe" or *th* in "thin," etc. (Bissex 1980). Mastery of these organizing principles requires ample exposure over time to their functions in print and opportunities to write independently. The latter possibility gives children a chance to use the print knowledge they are accumulating and to formulate and reformulate spelling strategies as they become available (Bissex 1980; Chomsky 1979).

Beginner writers, then, wrestle with segmenting the sounds of speech into discrete pieces or groups that can be represented by letters. Explorations of sound patterns in children's verbal art can enhance abilities to segment word sounds. Children can be asked to identify initial sounds in alliterative sequences ("Black Bears Burp"); or they can be invited to create their own versions of these tongue twisters. After being given adequate opportunities to appreciate and/or create phrases/sentences with words that rhyme, they can be encouraged to describe the sound patterns produced, that is, that rhyming words have different beginning sounds but the same end sounds, whereas alliterative sequences are, of course, the opposite. Such discussion opportunities can enhance children's awareness of the segmental as well as sequential nature of the sound structures of words. "The most advanced ability," Chomsky (1979) points out, "is segmenting the entire word into its component sounds" (55). The translation, however, from speech sounds to alphabetic systems is not direct, i.e., the three phonemes in the word "cat," for example, are heard as a continuous signal and not as separate sound units (Lieberman 1973). Hence the development of this level of segmenting ability appears to be greatly aided by exposure to print—that is, through reading and observing how phonemes function in the written representation of the sound/meaning features of spoken language (Chomsky 1979; Read 1978; Smith 1979).

Finally, how can the exploration of verse language contribute to children's efforts to master standard spelling? Let's take a look at common spelling patterns of words that rhyme:

> Twinkle, twinkle, little star,
> How I wonder what you are.
> Up above the world so high,
> Like a diamond in the sky.
> Twinkle, twinkle, little star,
> How I wonder what you are.

Verse language, because it is built upon patterns in sound, can focus children's attention on multiple relations which govern sound-to-spelling correspondences. Words that rhyme, as noted, have different beginning sounds but the same end sounds. This relation, though sometimes similarly represented in letter groups, is sometimes not (star/are; high/sky). The transcription of the phoneme /i/ in the latter pair exemplifies the same-sound/different-spelling pattern (number 1 above). This organizing principle is well represented in children's rhymes; thus the child's awareness of it is likely to be enhanced by opportunities to read and examine favorite verses.

Moreover, in written English, the same-sound/different-spelling pattern is especially characteristic of vowel transcriptions. Indeed, the long *e* sound has at least fifteen spellings: e, ie, ea, ee, e[]e, ei, ey, ay, eo, eau, i, i[]e, y, ae, and oe. Children of seven, eight, and nine are both astounded and intrigued by this fact. With a little provocation they can be inspired to "prove" it by searching for instances of every category. Or, operating inductively instead of deductively, youngsters can be invited to explore the following: "How many ways can you spell the long *a* sound [or any vowel] in our language?" A good place to begin "data collection" for this kind of search is in anthologies of verse where the use of rhyme, as noted, quite naturally exposes different ways to spell particular sound units.

Exploring the Literature

In addition to anthologies of verse (see Bibliography), there are many prose selections that incorporate wordplay. Among others, two prominent authors are listed whose children's stories are well loved both for their humorous language and for their comical development of characters and plot lines. They are A. A. Milne and Dr. Seuss. The Seuss stories are excellent examples of the "incongruity" humor so appealing to these ages. Bizarre descriptions of common items in the child's world *(Green Eggs and Ham)* as well as outlandish descriptions of happenings in the home *(The Cat in the Hat)* are presented in language carefully patterned to make the most of rhyme and meter.

A. A. Milne's *Winnie-the-Pooh* series tends to explore strategies of play—those derived from linguistic ambiguities—that are enjoyed by the older elementary ages. The central character, however, the bear named Winnie-the-Pooh, is, in thought and feeling, more like children in the early elementary years. Like many of the riddles which these ages repeat though they don't "understand" them, the Pooh books expose children to strategies of play which will become a part of their repertoire in a year or two.

There are also early readers that tell their tales in rhymes. Especially recommended are those authored by Dr. Seuss (there are over thirty) and Stan and Jan Berenstain (*The Big Honey Hunt* is one among many adventure stories about a family of bears). In becoming conversant with the differences among various styles, the child takes important steps toward understanding more about the world of words in books. Then, too, another important source of delightful reading material is Bill Martin, Jr.'s "Sounds of Language Readers," a series of books/anthologies of traditional and original stories in verse.

In considering selections to bring to a group, teachers may want to keep some additional criteria in mind. The first is, in a way, the crucial one: the selections must be enjoyed by both the teacher and the group. Teachers' tastes may not coincide with those of the children, and vice versa. The point is to find material that is enjoyable to both. Certainly, some selections may need a couple of airings with a group before one can tell if they are going to be welcomed. In the case of *Winnie-the-Pooh*, for instance, it may be necessary to read a few chapters before children are drawn into the story, become accustomed to the "wordy" prose, and begin to have some feeling for this whimsical bear.

Next, content should be within the real or imagined experience of these years. The prose and poetry of the writers cited in the bibliography often use animals as central characters. During these years most children continue to identify rather closely with animals and are still ready to enter into worlds in which animals talk like the human variety.

Frequently, as well, children's poetry uses wordplay as a means of describing animal attributes. Some particularly excellent examples are the poems by Mary Ann Hoberman (1973). In the following examples, she constructs a vivid word picture of a frog and a bee:

Frog

Pollywiggle	Wet Skin
Pollywog	Cold Blood
Tadpole	Squats in
Bullfrog	Mucky mud
Leaps on	Leaps on
Long legs	Long legs
Jug-o-rum	Jug-o-rum

Jelly eggs
Sticky tongue
Tricks flies
Spied by
Flicker eyes

Jelly eggs
Laid in
Wet bog . . .
Pollywiggle
Pollywog.

Bee

Who am I?
A big buzz
In a little fuzz.

In these examples, language play is used to describe not the antics of animals who behave like humans, but rather the attributes that define and separate them from others in the animal world. As noted, the use of language to describe and classify the stuff of the world is a skill children struggle to develop during these years. With these poems, children are exposed to descriptions enhanced by sound patterns representative of the animal or action described. Thus in the frog poem the meter suggests the frog's leaping motion as well as the swift motions of its tongue in catching food.

By way of summarizing this section it should be reiterated that because verse language is both familiar in content and predictable in form, it is extremely useful as a steady source of written language to which beginning reader/writers can be exposed. In addition to other continuous reading/writing efforts, these ages should be repeating, listening to, reading, and creating collections of favorite rhymes and verses in their classrooms, and not just outside of them.

The Middle
Elementary Years
(Eight through Eleven)

5 Language Play
in the Elementary Classroom

The encouraging of children's play as a pedagogical method generally forms a central part of programming for the early childhood ages. Program materials and schedules are carefully organized so that youngsters have opportunities to enact social scenarios and manipulate the stuff of the world as they move toward a better understanding of how social and physical things work. The framework for these experiences is that the adult constructs an environment in which youngsters can then make choices about where and how they will direct their explorations during work/play periods.

This tends not to be the case with the middle elementary ages. Here play is considered something youngsters engage in only outside the classroom. Moreover, language-learning activities, like those in the other disciplines, tend to be highly structured and focused on the teaching of particular skills. The bringing of language-play activities into such an environment, it has been argued, runs the risk of fatally eroding the spontaneity and therefore the usefulness of children's play. According to this view, teachers cannot take play opportunities— opportunities voluntarily engaged in—make them compulsory, and achieve creative and genuine results.

Such a position, however, does not give a complete picture, either of the kinds of play activities children engage in or the range of learning experiences that can be used in the classroom with these ages. It is during the years between seven and eleven that youngsters are inducted into the playing of games guided by specific sets of rules. At this point in their development, most children are becoming capable of understanding and submitting to rules of procedure which, rather than decreasing, enhance the pleasure and intensity of game playing. In the same way, wordplay forms—riddles, tongue twisters, humorous verses, etc.—have definite formulas that guide their invention. The question/answer frame of riddle rhetoric, the four-beat rhythm of most verses, and/or the back-and-forth repetition of knock-knocks, for example, define and characterize key play forms. The elementary ages, having been amply exposed to these forms, are approaching mastery of the particular discourse structures which govern them and appear to welcome opportunities to explore those structures both in and outside of the classroom.

A second and more serious charge regarding the bringing of wordplay into the elementary classroom is that some of its themes are not appropriate to be explored in this milieu. Many traditional verse forms are used to give expression to what is generally considered socially inexpressible. Often the content is subversive ("My eyes have seen the glory of the burning of the school . . ."); or hostile ("Roses are red / Violets are blue / Lemons are sour / And so are you"); or scatological ("Red, red / Wet the bed / Sop it up with gingerbread"). Unquestionably these types of verses represent a substantial part of the corpus of children's humorous poems. In fact their existence points to both children's need to express their resentments and the availability of verbal play to serve this need. Humorous language, youngsters are quick to grasp, has the advantage of reducing the speaker's responsibility for what he or she is saying, since the structure of the form (rhyme, meter, etc.) influences the choice and sequence of words. During the elementary years children begin to use jokes as a way of expressing what they ordinarily would not dare to say.

Personalized slurs directed at peers are also common. These often comment unfavorably on a physical characteristic: "Fatty, fatty, two by four / Can't get through the kitchen door." Or, they may be sexist: "Boys go to Mars / To eat candy bars / Girls go to Jupiter / To get much stupider." Frequently, youngsters challenge a newcomer to their class group by playing with the name, e.g., "Marty Miller" becomes "Farty Killer" (Nilsen 1983). Also, "tattletales"and "crybabies" are derided in rhymes because these behaviors tend not to be tolerated by these ages.

Then, too, ethnic and religious slurs find their way into the repertoires of fifth and sixth graders. "What is intriguing," Alvin Schwartz (1982) says, "is that most children who use the jokes don't have contact with the targets of these jokes." As Nilsen (1983) describes it, quoting Schwartz,

> "Then where do they learn that Poles are stupid, Italians are dirty, and Blacks are not to be trusted?" His answer is that they learn these things from the jokes which perpetuate themselves in a kind of scary circularity. "The joke teaches the stereotype. The stereotype provides a reason for telling the joke." (201)

The correction of such stereotypical thinking is a challenge to those of us who work with these ages.

Critics who argue that bringing wordplay to the classroom means encouraging hostile and antisocial exchanges have reversed the actual order of things. Wordplay is not the cause of this kind of behavior. Rather, it is simply one medium through which these impulses find expression. When antisocial behavior does erupt in the classroom—a common occurrence bearing no relation to investigations of wordplay—teachers censure it. It is a violation of classroom decorum and is not acceptable. If such behavior should occur in conjunction with a class exploration of wordplay, the adult response would be the same. Certainly, verbal play which becomes a part of the classroom activities and proceeds with not only the blessing but the active interest of the teacher must observe basic rules of social exchange. The idea is simply that rules which exist for other kinds of behavior would hold here as well.

Censure, however, is only part of the answer. The larger and much more important job is helping youngsters overcome their fear of peoples and customs that differ from the "norm," defined as the predominant ethnic group in the school population. A major part of the underground curriculum in classrooms of eight- to eleven-year-olds is the forming of attitudes toward people with varying backgrounds. It is "underground" because, though students frequently reveal their fears and prejudices both in the classroom and out of it, adults tend not to deal with these issues openly and directly. In fact, what needs to happen is that teachers cultivate as a part of their social studies programs during these years the appreciation and sharing of family origins, customs, differences, *and* similarities. Teachers can go a long way to offset the impulse to stereotype if they provide a forum for the sharing of everyone's "roots." In this kind of program an examination of humor that stereotypes can serve as the motivation for discussions about the cruelty and arbitrariness of such views. Students can certainly see the links between such jokes and the more common name-calling of these years. When not in the throes of an impulse to denigrate, these ages are quite capable of reflecting upon the pain inflicted by such epithets. They can, in fact, shift rapidly between "victor" and "victim" points of view, since they have all no doubt been in both positions. As Alleen Nilsen puts it, educating children to "go beyond stereotypes" requires much work. "But," she stipulates, "before we can help children, we have to lend an ear to what they are saying, even if it means hearing words that make us uncomfortable" (201).

Finally, the impulse to parody, call names, and/or demean can be redirected, for example, by active investigations of *appropriate* types of parody (see chapter 9). A consciousness of the inconsistencies and injustices of society makes its first appearance during these years. Such awareness can provide motivation for a critical evaluation of experience. The desire to blame can be usefully directed toward the creation of verbal lacerations of advertising or political absurdities and the like, which in our culture provide available and appropriate targets.

Opportunities for Play

Like those designing programs for five- to seven-year-olds, teachers of the middle elementary ages must think in terms of developing contexts for exploring wordplay. These can be characterized as providing three main types of teaching/learning experiences:

> *Appreciation* through the exploration of verbal play literature
>
> *Creation* through the presentation of opportunities to play with particular forms
>
> *Articulation* through the raising of questions regarding patterns of play

The differences in approach that these terms are meant to define are neither exclusive (there's a little of each in all of the approaches) nor strictly sequential in the sense that the development of a program would necessarily start with appreciation and work toward articulation. Each approach can be described, however, in terms of specific goals and activities that characterize it.

Appreciation refers not only to the bringing together of children and verbal play, but, what is more significant, to the bringing together of teachers' and children's delight in this activity. Elementary-age youngsters have enjoyed language play for generations, if not centuries. Its promulgation, as documented by the Opies, has been left largely in the hands of children, who faithfully pass an entire syllabus of riddles and jokes from one generation to the next. Only recently have certain humorists and writers collected and published significant amounts of the humorous verbal play particularly appealing to children in the elementary years. Such collections need to become part of the school or classroom library so that teachers and students alike can share their favorite examples with one another or their class group.

Types of spontaneous play specific to particular stages appear and disappear as children move through their school day. Thus, chanting, rhyming names of familiar people and places, and/or using routine jingles for "choosing up sides" make daily appearances in classrooms of the elementary years. In these classrooms *Mad* comics and their fac-similes also begin to make an appearance, and youngsters can be heard to share jokes specifically designed to poke fun at a current hero or well-known person.

A teacher's active appreciation, then, begins with remarking upon and enjoying these spontaneous expressions of play and, when appropriate, recording them for everyone to enjoy again and again. The idea is to begin to move children's verbal play into the regular channels of classroom exchange among children and adults.

In this sense, opportunities to appreciate language play will usually precede occasions to create. Ordinarily, teachers' choices of tasks with which to begin *creating* humorous language should derive from the assessment of what the group prefers to play or from students' current struggles with or discoveries of language systems (homophony, for example). The inclusion of topical themes as motivation to play can also help, very often, to stimulate more youngsters to play than only those who tend to be naturally so inclined.

Turning to *articulation*, it is useful to remember that all types of verbal play derive from the manipulation of specific sound/meaning relations of words and phrases. Children's articulation of these relations is sometimes spontaneous but more often a consequence of the teacher's questions. In providing opportunities to create or appreciate language play, teachers need to analyze the particular strategies involved. Once these are defined and within the teacher's conscious grasp, he or she can raise questions with children or groups of children as they become more experienced with verbal play. Depending upon the complexity of the patterns of play, final or complete answers should not be expected immediately from most children. Most youngsters need time to deliberate such questions, in conjunction with creating numerous examples of particular strategies or types of play, before they are ready to respond.

What are some common contexts for play and generally successful methods of exposure? First and most important is for teachers to pick up and capitalize upon clues from their class groups. All of the ways to elicit play described in these pages were chosen from possibilities in which children had already demonstrated an interest. At discussion times, for example, teachers may ask children to share favorite examples of a certain genre—riddles are one natural type around which to build verbal play sessions. One teacher of nine-year-olds built a humorous poetry session into her weekly program. She and the children would share new (or old) selections from literature that the teacher provided or examples of their own making. Sometimes another group was invited to join them and share favorites they had discovered.

Transition times—waiting in line or for an event to begin—are unfortunate but often unavoidable parts of group living. The sharing of jokes/riddles/knock-knocks also lend themselves to filling such moments pleasurably and easily.

As children become comfortable creating within certain types, these possibilities can become one of the choices for fulfilling writing assignments. In one school, a nine-year-old, David, began the year by flatly refusing to perform any writing assignments. It so happened that David was unusually able and interested in verbal play, a fact I had discovered from the verbal play sessions I had had with his class the previous year. When offered the possibility of fulfilling assignments by creating riddles or playing with literal/figurative expressions, he was delighted not only by the challenge of the activity but by the economy of the forms, that is, that there is so little physical writing to do! Little did he know that his composing abilities were actually being well exercised. Eventually, David would have to explore a variety of composing processes. Verbal play, however, helped him move into this area of literacy with a sense of confidence and fun, although far from being "easy" verbal play, like poetry, is characterized by economy of written expression and density of meaning. These forms thus offer children alternatives for writing assignments that are pleasurable not only because they involve humor but also because in form and organization they are so different from the demands presented by prose.

Among the many available books on language play those of two contributors deserve special mention. First, the collections of wordplay edited by Alvin Schwartz are especially delightful and appealing to these ages. Schwartz has made a point of compiling examples of humorous language inventions indigenous to America and American English. Like the Opies, he tends to bring a historical perspective to certain genres (e.g., tall tales and whoppers) as well as offering reasonable and delightful conjectures about the derivation of particular inventions. These descriptive asides are written for both children and adults to enjoy. What is presented, then, with these books is a compendium of American folklore as expressed through verbal play. And, besides the very famous and very humorous *Alice in Wonderland*, by Lewis Carroll, there is, among other of the more ambitious selections of humorous prose, a relatively recent addition by Norton Juster called *The Phantom Tollbooth*. This book is, from one point of view, an exploration of just how many ways one might play with structures, definitions, and anomalies found not only in language but in mathematics and its systems of numbers as well. Most children in the eight-to-eleven age range will enjoy at least one encounter with this book; many will want to read and reread it. It is an especially good choice to read aloud, since it provides numerous opportunities to discuss the humorous use of words and numbers as well as normal and "abnormal" uses of these symbols that constitute so much of the plot material.

Finally, the importance of keeping intact the "wholeness" of children's response to play opportunities cannot be overemphasized. Critics who argue that the integrity of children's impulse to play can be undermined in what tends to be the highly structured, "skill-drill" environment of the elementary classroom are justified if such activities are used as out-of-context methods for teaching punctuation, grammar, vocabulary, and so on. Indeed, children's language play provides excellent evidence in support of the case for the holistic nature of language learning. Wordplay, by definition, intrigues because it explores language forms and functions *at the same time* that it gives vent to humorous impulses. As types of play described in the next chapters reveal, the repeating and sharing of specific wordplay comes first. Only after certain types have been amply laughed over and delighted in do they become natural sources for exploring the way words work.

6 Wrinkles in the Language Code

Especially significant about children's wordplay in the middle elementary years is the complex perspective on language explored in youngsters' expanding ways of playing, e.g., taunts and teases, puns, parodies, knock-knocks, and a variety of riddle forms. Through the medium of play, third through sixth graders explore apparent inconsistencies in the language code. Well along on the road of language learning, these ages understand that the basic function of verbal exchange is to give reasonably clear descriptions of experience. Ambiguous interpretations, should they arise, must be corrected to favor a single meaning. However, the code provides numerous ways of introducing confusions in communication. This seeming contradiction, or "wrinkle" as McDowell (1979) calls it, provides these ages with many opportunities for play.

The Principle of Parsimony

Eight-year-old Frank stopped me in the hall one day and posed the following riddle, "What state is like a small soft drink?" When I couldn't come up with the answer, Frank announced with delight, "Mini-soda!" To insure my full appreciation of this bit of verbal wit, Frank then elaborated the sound/meaning/spelling similarities and differences between "Minnesota" and "mini-soda." In an earlier example, I described six-year-old Sarah's discovery that certain words sound the same (crow/Crowe) but have different meanings (bird/surname). For Frank and others his age, homophones provide a nearly endless source of material for play through juxtaposing multiple meanings for a single phrase in verses and riddles: "If we cantaloupe / Lettuce marry . . ." or, "Why did the cookie cry?" (Because its mother was a wafer so long).

What has been unearthed by our players is the "principle of parsimony" that characterizes the sound system of our language code (McDowell 1979). There are thousands of words in our language but only forty-four separate sound units with which to express them, with the result that many words and phrases sound the same or similar to other words/phrases, i.e., there is frequent use of the same sound sequence to represent separate lexical items.

Common categories of homophones that tend to be encountered in the verbal play of these ages are:

1. Words with identical sounds (and/or spellings) and different meanings:
    a. Proper nouns and common nouns:
    Mark: proper name
    mark: a spot, or a grade
    b. Words with different derivations:
    to lie (OE. *licgan*): to be in a horizontal position
    to lie (OE. *leogan*): to deceive
    c. Words with different spellings and meanings but identical pronunciations:
    red: a color
    read: past tense of the verb "to read"
    (Other examples common in the vocabularies of elementary children are *way/weigh; pear/pair/pare; flower/flour; there/their/they're.*)

2. Sound identities between letter names and words:
    "b": letter name
    to be: the intransitive verb meaning to exist
    bee: name for an insect that stings and produces honey
    (Other examples are *c/see/sea; g/gee; i/eye; k/Kay; p/pee/pea; r/are/our; t/tea/tee; u/you; y/why.*)

3. Instances wherein word boundaries are confused:
    a. A word whose syllables can offer another meaning:
    lettuce: a vegetable
    let us: permit us
    b. The shifting of boundaries between words to suggest another meaning:
    eight tea cups: a specific number of cups for tea
    eighty cups: a much larger number of cups of any kind

This list, while hardly exhaustive, indicates how numerous the instances of homophony are in the English language. It is just this condition of language that middle elementary youngsters confront in their struggle to master English orthography. In a story, for example, written by ten-year-old Mark, these substitutions appeared: "hear" for "here"; "herd" for "heard"; "tern" for "turn"; and "board" for "bored." He knew perfectly well the meaning he intended, but he had not yet mastered spelling variations. As a help in correcting these mistakes, Mark needed to be alerted to lexical features that motivate standard spellings.

Homophone lists, so often found in classrooms of third through sixth graders, can provide an excellent source of wordplay material. In addition to the riddles of the "mini-soda" type, the cartoon caption form can provide a neat juxtaposition of the same-sound/different-meaning pattern (fig. 5). And as youngsters move into the later elementary grades, they should have opportunities not only to expand their homophone lists but to categorize the word pairs according to source and type. Such activities provide excellent exercises in understanding sound/meaning/spelling relations among words.

Metaphor and Meaning

All parents and teachers have noted the "literalness" that invades the eight- or nine-year-old's language interpretations. When asked to

Figure 5. "Knight on a horse"

"pick up his room," my son, eight, delighted in staggering about as if shouldering an enormous load. Such literal interpretations of figurative expressions are proof of yet another important discovery about the nature of language: that it is full of words and phrases with multiple, metaphorically related meanings.

In the last twenty years some especially good books for stimulating such explorations have been published. Among these are the "Amelia Bedelia" series by Peggy Parish, and Fred Gwynne's books *(The King Who Rained; Chocolate Moose)*. Youngsters I've worked with in the eight-to-eleven age range found these books hilarious. The characters have a penchant for producing literal interpretations of figurative expressions, shown in a picture/caption format. When asked to "dress the chicken," for example, Amelia, a domestic worker, is pictured attiring it in shorts and socks.

With the Parish or Gwynne books as models the youngsters in the eight-to-eleven age range I have worked with have enjoyed producing literal interpretations of figurative expressions (figs. 6 and 7). The captions tend to be either one or two words—"Shop Lifting," "Nuthead," "Footnote"—or complete phrases/sentences—"You took the words right out of my mouth," "I'm blue," "My feet are killing me," "I'm up to my ears in paper." The pictures exploit one or more of the concrete references embedded in these idioms. This phenomenon can be described as these ages' particular penchant for resurrecting dead metaphors.

This phenomenon, well documented in children's traditional word-play literature, can be related to the middle elementary youngster's developing grasp of structures of meaning. The phrase "dead metaphor" has been used to describe the metaphoric evolution of word meanings (Burke 1945; Cassirer 1953; Lakoff and Johnson 1980; Langer 1951; Vygotsky [1934] 1962). Over the centuries, these thinkers point out, new objects and ideas take their place on the roster of human experience by being granted a name. The naming process can be described as one of juxtaposing known and unknown through metaphoric creations. The word "neck," for example, initially a name for that part of the body that joins the head and torso, refers, in present-day nomenclature, to similar jointures such as the "neck" of a hammer or bottle. Then, too, a certain type of traffic jam is called a "bottle-neck." The metaphoric extension of the name is based on the recognition that some but not all properties represented by that word/name are similar to those of other objects/actions. This metaphoric extension of meaning, however, once accepted and integrated into daily exchange, is no longer noted. The initial recognition of relations

Figure 6. "Shop lifting"

Figure 7. "I'm up to my ears in paper."

between different domains fades ("dies," as it were) and the use of these words/phrases evokes only their figurative meaning. This is true for most adult speakers—our middle elementary youngsters, however, gleefully resurrect dead metaphors in their wordplay.

In terms of the acquisition process, the awareness that a single word or phrase can have multiple meanings begins to make an appearance around kindergarten age. Thus five-year-old Rebecca, commenting to her father about a man she had seen with only one leg, was told that "he must have lost the other one." Her puzzled response to this explanation was "You can't lose a leg." Rebecca's grasp of meanings for the verb "to lose" did not yet include the amputation of a limb. The fact, though, that she is alert to and comments upon what to her is an anomalous use of the verb is evidence of a first step in coming to grips with metaphoric extension of meanings for words/phrases. Nine-year-old Jenny, on the other hand, laughingly recounted to me how she used to think that "putting on lipstick" meant applying something that would seal ("stick") the lips—a confusion that she had since cleared up. It is, indeed, in the years between five and nine that most youngsters begin to appreciate metaphoric extensions of meaning in language.

Further, in terms of the development of metaphoric competence, the resurrecting of dead figures of speech involves processes similar to those engaged in the construction of live examples. To return to the play examples recorded at the beginning of this section, the productions highlight the fact that certain words/phrases name more than one class of objects/actions (their extensions) and, as a result, represent more than one set of attributes (their intensions). The play strategy revolves around the misalliance of extension and intension. Witness this misalliance in the "Shop Lifting" example:

	to lift
extensions	*intensions*
to raise	bringing to a higher position
to steal	taking property from a store

In playing with the phrase "shop lifting" the child inappropriately pairs the extension "to raise" with the intension "taking property from a store." To produce these kinds of juxtapositions, the creator is called upon to perform an analysis of some part of the range of extensions and intensions represented by the idiom under scrutiny. The exercise is one of recovering—speculating about, in a sense—the property or attribute that prompted the metaphoric extension of the name in the first place. From this point of view, it would appear that in their play youngsters are examining one of the bases of metaphoric creation: *that an attribute representative of one class of ideas or experiences can be analogously represented in other domains.*

Vocabulary study in elementary language programs can easily incorporate play with the resurrection of dead metaphors. Along with riddle play of this type (see chapter 7), the way I have worked with class groups is to follow the reading of one of the Gwynne or Parish books with a discussion in which youngsters are invited to search for similar possibilities for play. After this kind of brainstorming, I pass out drawing materials and have youngsters record their own creations in cartoon/caption format. Such sessions have been almost uniformly successful. There was always much delight in hearing the books, and the discussion usually elicited a plethora of idioms for which youngsters would give a literal interpretation to be represented in pictures. As is often the case, the discussion period tended to be dominated by the more playful and verbal members of the age group; however, the ideas of these youngsters and their modeling of how to approach this task helped to release the playful capacities of the more cautious ones. In each of the class groups the creations were matted and put into a class book. A title was selected and the final anthology became a part of the class library.

In addition to these creations derivative of play with dead metaphors, there were offerings by youngsters who preferred to reproduce an example from one of the model books. These were youngsters who were either unable or unwilling to attempt their own creations. Their appreciation of this kind of play, however, was indicated in their reconstructions of favorite examples.

This activity seemed to generate greatest involvement when a series of play sessions was scheduled over a period of weeks. It appears that once the ground had been prepared, so to speak, and youngsters alerted to search for idioms with which to play, most began to "hear" these words/phrases with increasing frequency in everyday exchanges. In between scheduled sessions, youngsters were encouraged to record these words/phrases on a chart on one of the bulletin boards so that they would be available at the next play session.

7 The Rigors of Riddling

History tells us that riddling is nearly as ancient as civilization itself. Humankind, it appears, has long enjoyed the use of this form of verbal rhetoric to challenge and to tease, to engage its members in contests of mental rather than physical prowess. Very likely, it is this safe channeling of aggressive impulses that also attracts children to riddling (Wolfenstein [1954] 1978). But whatever the motivation, one observes that efforts at riddling dominate the informal verbal play of children during their elementary years. One also observes that this activity, which offers many possibilities for learning, has been largely ignored in our elementary school classrooms.

Implicit in the following descriptions is the assumption that riddles and riddling constitute an important part of the classroom exchange among students and adults. The elementary years are a time when with little or no preparation the teacher can suggest that youngsters hold a riddling session. Such sessions might function as transition games or even as scheduled weekly sessions wherein youngsters can share their latest examples. As early as six years of age, many youngsters begin to commit riddles to memory. Their accumulated repertoire of traditional examples as well as the additions that will accrue from opportunities to create their own can provide ample material to fill these sessions.

In the riddle analyses that follow, I outline four major strategies this form exploits. These guidelines for classroom riddle production propose methods for helping youngsters to differentiate these patterns of play as well as to create within them.

Producing Fresh Metaphors

With this strategy, children create riddles whose obscurities derive from the posing of a cryptic or unusual description of a common object or action:

1. What are polka dots on your face?
   (Pimples)

In creating riddles derived from this strategy, the process involves the joining of disparate elements of experience through the perception (and description) of their resemblances. In addition to the example cited above, the Opies have recorded numerous examples of children's metaphoric riddle rhymes:

2. Riddle me, riddle me
    riddle me ree,
   I saw a nut cracker
    up in a tree.
        (A squirrel)

3. White and thin, red within,
   With a nail at the end.
        (A finger)

4. Neither flesh or neither bone
   Yet it had four fingers and a thumb.
        (A glove)

In formulating opportunities to create metaphoric riddles, it is helpful to identify key aspects of the process as they are represented in children's productions. Like the descriptive riddles in which children present attributes and then request that the listener identify the object to which they belong, these metaphoric productions reveal children's continued exploration of how a thing might be defined. For example, in 2 above an identity is proposed between the object in question and answer; in 3 above the question enumerates attributes of the object named in the answer; and in 4 above the question enumerates attributes (defines) a hand, only some of which are representative of a glove.

Previous descriptions of opportunities to create riddles have emphasized the utility of identifying word examples that lend themselves to riddle exploitation. Once particular possibilities have been collected and recorded, children can concentrate on how to distribute objects and attributes between question and answer. With metaphoric productions, youngsters who may have difficulties approaching the renaming process might be helped by the following instructions:

> Choose an item in the room and consider it in light of the following questions:
>
> What does it remind you of?
>
> How might you describe this thing?
>
> What do the descriptions make you think of?

A child might choose the class pet—a turtle—as the object of the riddle solution. The fact that the turtle's shell is its "house" is often a significant feature of this animal in children's eyes. This information lends itself well to the construction of metaphorical riddles:

> I carry my house around with me.
> Who am I?

> If my house is upside down
> Then I cannot move around.
> Who am I?

The suggestion is that in helping children to create riddles of this type, it is easier to begin with a form similar to the descriptive riddles in which the features of an item—imaginatively presented—are allowed to symbolize the item in the answer as in 3 above and the "turtle" examples. Proposing an identity between two things as in 1 and 2 would be a next step. Many youngsters, though, readily explore renaming possibilities given the stimulus of only one word. From there, they are perfectly capable of defining and distributing objects and/or attributes in appropriate riddle rhetoric.

In providing opportunities to articulate aspects of this riddle form, the children's own productions often offer the best source of examples. The children's responses, moreover, to any of the riddling discussions should offer clues to teachers regarding a child's level of development of certain skills, for example, to what extent they grasp the relationships among sets of attributes for words with metaphorically related meanings and to what extent they can articulate differences between defining and nondefining attributes of word concepts. The clarity and expressiveness of verbal communication—whether written or spoken—is in part dependent upon the command of an increasing quantity of words as well as the conceptual frameworks they represent. The emphasis on vocabulary development, then, and grasp of meaning in the elementary years is certainly deserved and could well be enhanced by explorations of this riddle type.

Resurrecting Dead Metaphors

Like the cartoon/caption form, the riddle provides an excellent frame for examining metaphorically related meanings of single words or phrases.

1. What has an eye but cannot see?
   (A needle, potato, storm, etc.)

2. What did the rug say to the floor?
(I've got you covered.)

The strategy in the first example exploits the fact that the attributes specified in the question and answer have the same name but not the same sets of defining features. In the second riddle, the strategy is to propose a literal interpretation for a figurative expression. Examples derived from these riddle formulas are legion in the wordplay repertoires of these ages. And their examination can serve as a source of study of metaphoric extensions of meaning. For example, students can be asked to create (on their own or as a group) entries for the formula: What has a _____ but cannot _____ ? A _____ . As examples accumulate they can be recorded on a chart:

Question Entries	Answer Entries
eye . . . see	needle, potato, storm
leg . . . walk	table, chair, journey
teeth . . . chew	comb, saw

After their investigation via creation, students will be ready to articulate aspects of word meanings exemplified by these groups: (1) What is the relation between word pairs in the question entries?; and (2) What are similarities/differences among entries in each of the answer categories?

A similar exploration can be carried out with the second riddle formula. Here youngsters are given the chance to examine dead metaphors in our language. Like the "Shop Lifting" example, an examination of relations between literal and figurative meanings as highlighted in the riddle format can enhance youngsters' understanding of metaphoric connections between these semantic frames. Further, by the time youngsters get to be ten and eleven they are eager for and quite capable of speculation about: (1) Which came first, literal or figurative meanings for these words/phrases? Why? and (2) Why are actions/experiences so named? These types of discussions offer students the chance to reflect upon relations between language growth and human perceptions. Teachers can introduce terminology such as "metaphoric," or "literal/figurative" as they see fit. What needs to be borne in mind is that no attempt should be made to instruct children in these concepts through the premature introduction of these terms and their definitions. Rather, riddles that exploit these linguistic systems provide an arena wherein children can articulate these ideas within the specific frame of reference provided by the play experience.

With this series of tasks, it is wise to expect differences in response between eight-year-olds and, say, a group of sixth graders. For the eight-year-olds, certain introductory tasks may prove to be sufficiently comprehensive as an area of exploration. The grouping of riddles into different patterns as well as the detection and exploration of words that name different classes of objects involves a great deal of classifying and thinking about language.

The process for helping youngsters derive patterns of riddles can be described as follows:

1. Teacher begins by grouping examples familiar to the class (e.g., those derived from play with multiple related meanings of words or those representative of riddle parody, described below).

2. Children are invited to study the group and describe the pattern(s); eight-year-olds may need to take one type at a time, while older youngsters can compare and contrast riddle patterns.

3. Riddles of a certain pattern can be posted on charts in the room and the children invited to find other examples of that pattern.

4. Finally, children can be given a series of riddles and invited to do their own grouping.

Along with these kinds of opportunities, youngsters can be encouraged to "create" a riddle book by choosing to reproduce riddles representative of a particular pattern.

On the other hand, within a single discussion, some sixth-grade classes may be able to define and explore a riddle formula, as well as the sources of words it tends to exploit, to produce their own examples of that formula, and to discuss the nature of metaphorical extension of meaning in language. For an assignment, they might choose two or three riddle formulas and propose five or more appropriate entries for each.

Finally, the significance of this metaphoric structure of word meanings should become more and more apparent to youngsters as they begin to detect its presence in the naming and defining of concepts related to, say, their science and social studies work. Metaphoric perceptions—that is, the recognition of similarities among differences—and the use of these perceptions to extend the use of a word-name to include more than one class of objects represents a particular semantic structure, knowledge of which can become a practical tool for building vocabulary. The issue becomes not just understanding a significant structure in the design of language but also comprehending new and unfamiliar concepts and experiences. Familiar words, or parts of words such as prefixes, appearing in new contexts alert youngsters to recall meanings previously associated with these words and to search for ways in which these meanings might be applicable in the new situation.

Exploiting Homophones

Examples of this type of riddle strategy are:

1. What is black and white and re(a)d all over?
   A newspaper.
2. Why will you never starve in the desert?
   Because of the sandwiches there.

As noted in the previous chapter, ambiguities derived from homophonic structures are a result of the limited number of separate sound units from which the thousands of words in our language are made up. Also noted was the fact that by the time youngsters reach the third grade (if not before), they have begun to struggle with the results of this feature of our language in their spelling. As a way of highlighting and, as a result, helping to remedy the problems, children can be encouraged to encode these word pairs in a riddle frame.

Riddles that exploit this structure are abundant because of the many English words that are the same or similar in sound but have different derivations, meanings, and/or spellings. Some examples are:

Why did the jam roll?
Because it saw the apple turnover.
(Nouns perform as verbs)

What has four wheels and flies?
A garbage truck.
("Flies" meaning the insects/"flies" as third person singular of the verb to fly)

When does a letter sting?
When it's a bee.
(Sound identities between word-names)

In exploring riddles of these types, children can be invited to describe similarities and differences among these homophones. In preparing, certainly, to create riddles of this type, children need opportunities to record and classify words/phrases that represent homophonic patterns.

Children who have explored riddles derived both from homophones and from words with metaphorically related meanings may be ready for an opportunity to compare these structures. Examples of each which the group has explored in riddle form can be juxtaposed:

Homophones	*Single Words with Multiple Meanings*
red (the color)	eye (of a person)
read (to have read a book)	eye (of a needle)
b (letter name)	to cover (to place something on or
bee (the insect)	over)
	to cover (to point a firearm at)

Children can be invited to respond to questions that help them focus on ways of comparing these word pairs:

Their sound relationships

Their meaning relationships

Their similarities and differences as representative patterns of sound/meaning systems in our language

Riddle Parodies

In the middle and later elementary years parody forms—poems, riddles, and the transposition of well-known titles or labels—flourish. Riddle parodies derive their name from the fact that, unlike the paradoxical formulations usual to riddles, these riddle answers propose straightforward solutions to the riddle question:

Why did the chicken cross the road?

To get to the other side.

The creation of these productions should not pose any difficulties. The challenge is to time their appearance in a riddling session so that the riddlees don't anticipate or guess the riddler's strategy. Because its strategy is in fact the opposite of that of most riddles, the riddle parody provides an excellent foil for the identification of usual riddle strategies. In comparing and contrasting examples of each type children have an opportunity to define the nature of riddle incongruities, reversals, contradictions, and/or straightforward solutions.

Riddling in the Classroom

Early in the school year, a mixed group of ten- and eleven-year-olds that I met with weekly was exposed to opportunities for verbal play as a result of my interest in gathering data on children's humorous language. As a result of my participation, verbal play became an accepted and valued part of our daily exchange. It set the stage, so to speak, for children and teacher to search for more ways to play. Later in the year, I introduced the group to the "hink-pink" riddle form. Quickly, a riddling session emerged. About a third of the youngsters immediately became engaged in the exploration of these new possibilities for verbal dueling, while the rest of the group, including the teacher, listened with rapt attention. By way of describing the hink-pink form, let's take a look at three creations by these youngsters:

1. What do you call a naughty kid when he grows up?
   (A bad dad)
2. What do you call a complete and accurate part of a state?
   (A thorough borough)
3. What do you call it when a general makes a mistake on his plans?
   (A strategy tragedy)

Formally, the outstanding characteristic of this riddle type is that the words in the solution must rhyme and be in meter. This latter aspect of the riddle is indicated by the riddler, who, when sharing his or her creation, prefaces asking the riddle question by declaring that it will be a "hink-pink," meaning that each word in the solution has a single syllable, as in 1 above; a "hinky-pinky," indicating two syllables, as in 2; or a "hinkety-pinkety," indicating three syllables, as in 3.

With regard to content, these constructions represent an exercise in the descriptive use of language. It is more or less understood that the identity of the item is announced in the question; the real challenge, then, the requirement that the answer be in rhyme and in meter, stretches the student's linguistic creativity and originality. Thus while "strategy tragedy" is a novel locution for describing military errors, its aptness should be as obvious as is its young creator's wit.

The students' initial creations were admired, shared, and posted on a hink-pink chart in the room. As the weeks passed everyone began contributing to this class hink-pink "anthology." One youngster, Tom, figured out that this form provided an excellent substitute for the obligatory weekly writing of sentences for new vocabulary words. Tom, who did not like writing sentences, turned out to be a hink-pink wizard. In the sample of his productions below (note that the class was involved in a study of medieval history), the vocabulary word is italicized:

1. What do you call a sad *gargoyle?*
   (A pout spout)

2. What do you call a servant who works in the center aisle of a church?
   (A *nave* slave)

3. When two people sign a peace treaty and they drink to it, what do they drink?
   (*Truce* juice)

While most of the students could not create with Tom's skill and inventiveness, all were eventually intrigued by the possibilities of this riddle form and nearly everyone's vocabulary sentences were slowly infiltrated by hink-pinks and their derivatives. Indeed, the form is a good method for exploring word meanings, because the juxtaposition of words/phrases in the question parts and their answers requires precision in differentiating the meanings of words.

The range of riddling competence in this group of fourteen students included four youngsters who could perform on a par with Tom and, at the other end of the continuum, another group of four whose interest and appreciation of these creations probably surpassed their capacity for production:

1. What is the opposite of subtraction innovation?
   (Addition *tradition*)

2. What do you call a faint large sickness that kills many?
   (A vague *plague*)

3. What do you call a 1/16-of-a-pound jump?
   (An *ounce* pounce)

4. What did someone do when she called 1/60 of a minute?
   (She beckoned to a *second*.)

In this final group of samples from the less able riddlers, the reader will note that questions are contrived, while, in the answers, rhyme and meter are not often violated. Apparently the formal structure of the solution is easier to master than the more sophisticated framing of the question.

8 Humorous Verse

In the repertoire of play strategies, the one most often referred to and generally admired (by wordplayers) is the perfect pun:

Many a blonde $\begin{cases} \text{dies} \\ \text{dyes} \end{cases}$ by her own hand . . .

Such constructions require that a single phonological phrase/sentence have two distinct meanings. The production and comprehension of such jokes, however, is beyond the powers of most middle elementary youngsters. Seven- to eleven-year-olds explore creations known as "imperfect" puns—constructions in which one similar-sounding word/phrase is humorously substituted for another (geometry/gee, I'm a tree; canoe/can you). Children's first encounters with these kinds of constructions tend to be through the memorizing and repeating of "knock-knocks." Two typical examples are:

"Knock, knock."
"Who's there?"
"Butcher."
"Butcher who"
"Butcher feet on the floor."

"Knock, knock."
"Who's there?"
"Isabelle."
"Isabelle who?"
"Isabelle ringing?"

The punning technique of using a word once as a whole and then in parts is a form children in the early elementary years are able to appreciate. In the first appearance of the pun, it is a proper or generic name. Subsequently the name is broken into syllables or additional syllables are added to suggest an entirely different meaning, a phrase or clause. The distortions in the pronunciation of the pun in its second appearance do not distress these ages or detract from the humor of the joke for them. In fact, children are most often delighted by what they perceive as the incongruity of a sound similarity—crude though it may be—between words and phrases with unrelated meanings.

Another example children enjoy is a poem in which numerous strategies for punning (imperfectly) are explored:

> Do you carrot all for me?
> My heart beets for you.
> With your turnip nose,
> And your radish face
> You are a peach.
> If we cantaloupe,
> Lettuce marry,
> Weed make a swell pear.

The humor of the verse derives from the fact that names belonging to one semantic domain—vegetables—have been used to describe another—emotions. In terms of humorous form, this device is a type of parody in which the incongruities derive from descriptions of the spiritual in terms of the material. As in the knock-knocks, the comparatively gross differences in the pronunciation of the vegetable name and its pun rendition do not trouble children; a crude similarity between the two is adequate, especially since the puns serve the general thematic development of love in terms of vegetables.

Another strategy for suggesting multiple meanings of single words is the use of homophones—the type that are identical in pronunciation but have different derivations:

> beets : beats
>
> weed : we'd
>
> pear : pair

In this group of puns, as in the first, these vegetable names (nouns) often function in the wrong grammatical categories—that is, as verbs and adjectives. This, however, is frequently the case with puns, whose "working" requires a willingness to suspend for the moment the application of rules of grammar.

The final strategy employed in this poem is the use of the word "peach"—correctly—in its metaphoric sense of sweet or pleasing. In this context, though, we are immediately reminded of the fruit itself, the literal meaning of the word.

During these years the penchant for creating imperfect puns derives in part from the necessity to absorb at a fairly rigorous pace an extensive vocabulary of unfamiliar names of equally unfamiliar people and places:

> Mississippi said to Missouri,
> "If I put on my New Jersey
> What will Delaware?"
> Virginia said, "Alaska" . . .

Or, as in this example from the Opies' collection (1959):

> Austria was Hungary
> Took a bit of Turkey
> Dipped it in Greece
> Fried it in Japan
> And ate it off China.

Because the names, as proper names, have few if any associations for children, they readily transpose these items into what is to them a meaningful utterance. It is their way of making the unfamiliar familiar. But whether or not the reference is familiar or unfamiliar, what intrigues is the discovery that one word or phrase can, with a little distortion in pronunciation, allow for another meaning.

Examples of this type of play should be shared among members of a class group. The memorizing and repeating of knock-knocks and verse forms that exploit imperfect puns will prompt some children to begin creating their own examples. Most children will be aided in their efforts by some conscious detection and experimentation with words and phrases which lend themselves to these kinds of transpositions. Their discoveries can be recorded and used as a resource for possibilities with which to formulate their own knock-knocks or verses. Children should be encouraged to articulate patterns of transposition:

> The breaking of a word or phrase into syllables (cantaloupe/can't elope)
>
> The shifting of word boundaries (a wafer/away for)

As is the nature of learning, the articulation of these patterns will prompt some children to explore deductively, i.e., take a pattern and apply it systematically to words and phrases they encounter.

As the examples suggest, one way of organizing children's creation of imperfect puns is to choose a particular semantic category to explore—one that is related to a current unit of study. When enough possibilities have been recorded, inventions of one, two, or more lines can be created by the group or individual students. The invention of verse forms—especially those of more than one stanza—offers excellent opportunities for a group to invent together.

Limericks

> A duck whom I happened to hear
> Was complaining sadly, "Oh dear,
>   Our picnic's today
>   But the weathermen say
> That the skies will be sunny and clear!"

Children in this age range may not know this form by name, but they are generally familiar with particular examples. Moreover, they can often recapitulate in nonsense syllables the meter and stanza form:

da - DA - da - da - DA - da - da - DA

Preliminary to the creation of their own, and after an acquaintance with traditional examples, children can be invited to articulate the obvious and consistent features of this form:

Anapestic meter

Five-line stanza (three long and two short)

An *aabba* rhyme scheme

Incongruities (derived from puns, polysemy and/or the incongruous reversal of accepted notions, as in the above example)

While many youngsters may have difficulty controlling all of these features in their inventions, they can generally produce something that is unmistakably a limerick. The following examples were produced by two eight-year-old girls:

There once was a silly little frog
Who lived in a most hideous bog
    The dust and the smoke
    Always made him choke
And that's all about the frog.

There was a young rabbit from Turkey
Who had a friend snake with a smile so smirky
    She asked him for tea
    But he said, "Not me,
I have to go to worky."

Once again, group efforts are often a good way to begin. Poets develop, as part of their craft, a range of ways to fulfill the demands of a particular form. Similarly, a group of children could draw on the larger resources of all its members to meet the requirements of the form.

Finally, this form provides an excellent introduction to key elements of the formal patterning of language found in most poems. Rhyme, rhythm, and special requirements for presenting meanings are clearly identified.

Tongue Twisters

As noted earlier, tongue twisters have traditionally intrigued youngsters because of the challenge to their powers of pronunciation.

Phrases such as "aluminum linoleum" and "Unique New York" are to be repeated (five or ten times) with speed and clarity. Everyone wants to try—it sounds so easy—but few succeed. As popular are the lengthier twisters:

> How many cans can a canner can
> If a canner can can cans?
> A canner can can as many cans
> As a canner can
> If a canner can can cans.

Always eager to propose a contest in which he was likely to be the victor, my son would lure me into competing in speedy repetitions of such verses. He, who like most children his age would spend hours practicing a twister, was indeed always the winner. Again, after making these verbal exercises a part of classroom exchanges teachers can help children to talk about what they have no doubt intuited about the word "can" (and many others like it in our language): that it possesses an unusual flexibility in its uses. Two similar examples of this type of tongue twister popular with eight- and nine-year-olds are:

> Of all the saws I ever saw saw,
> I never saw a saw saw that could saw
> As this saw saws.

> How much wood would a woodchuck chuck
> If a woodchuck could chuck wood?
> A woodchuck would chuck as much wood
> As a woodchuck could chuck,
> If a woodchuck could chuck wood.

With these types of tongue twisters, children can be invited to articulate the multiple participation in systems of meaning and syntax of which many words are capable:

> They can function as verbs or nouns.

> Many have identical sounds but different derivations, or different developments of the same derivation, and therefore different meanings.

> Different suffixes (or prefixes) can give different meanings to the same root word.

Children can be encouraged to search for and record other words that fit all or some of these categories.

Some twisters are constructed in limerick form:

> A flea and a fly in a flue
> Were imprisoned, so what could they do?

"Let us fly," said the flea.
"Let us flee," said the fly.
So they flew through a flaw in the flue.

Again, with this example, youngsters can be invited to describe what makes this verse (and others) a tongue twister. As they begin to formulate ideas about the use of words having the same or similar sounds, their descriptions, with examples, can be recorded. Common word categories appearing in tongue twisters are: (1) homophones (flee/flea; wood/would); (2) words that rhyme (flue/flew/do/through); and (3) words derived from a common root (a "fly"/to "fly"). This kind of exploration might lead as well to a study of the influence of word meaning and/or derivation on spelling patterns. And again, in examining instances of category 3 above, children can explore the grammatical flexibility of words in our language.

In creating their own examples, many children will find that the construction of a "sensible" sequence of phrases that exploits this source of words is a demanding task. Twisters in verse form are more easily constructed when the strategy derives from alliteration, as in the "Sleepy Sailboat" story cited earlier and the "Sea Shell" favorite recorded below:

She sells sea shells at the sea shore,
At the sea shore she sells sea shells.
And if she sells sea shells at the sea shore,
The sea shells she sells are sea shore shells,
Of that I'm sure.

The students' command of this type of sound pattern as well as the greater quantity of words from which to choose tends to make this type easier to construct. Also, children should note that in most verse-length tongue twisters, words, phrases, and even entire lines are repeated. The creator simply contrives a transition which requires that what was said before be repeated, i.e., "*And if* she sells sea shells at the sea shore . . ."

Tangle Talk

The following examples of tangle talk, repeated years ago by me and my eight-year-old friends, continue to be favorites of the current elementary school generation:

Ladies and Gentlemen
I come before you
To stand behind you

To tell you what I know nothing about
Pull up a chair
And sit on the floor
Admission is free
Pay at the door.

'Twas a summer day in winter
And the snow was raining fast;
As a barefoot boy, with shoes on,
Stood sitting on the grass.

There are not, as in most other verse categories, a more or less unlimited number of examples of this type. And in the selections which I have examined, there is a remarkable resemblance among the themes explored. As in the above examples, designations of time, position, climate, dress, and demeanor are all explored through the juxtaposition of contradictory phrases. In making up their own examples, children can be encouraged either to follow the thematic development of a model—making their own substitutions for time designations, etc.—or to formulate their own sequences on these or other themes. This type of verse, observe Sanches and Kirshenblatt-Gimblett, "calls attention to semantic rules of co-occurrences by violating them" (1976, 100). In the process of achieving mastery of this structure, children delight in exploring instances wherein the rules appear to be functioning correctly but in fact are not.

Children's Verbal Art

Elementary school youngsters, like the nursery and primary ages, explore specific linguistic structures through the medium of humorous verse. In this later stage, strategies of play derive most often from the exploitation of relations among sound and meaning systems of language. Homophones, imperfect puns, and the literal interpretation of figurative expressions are variations on a single linguistic theme. What intrigues eight- to eleven-year-olds is how many ways sound and sense can be manipulated to form unexpected results. Moreover, the exploration of rhetorical frames, however repetitive and elementary, points to the close connection between wordplay and the development of poetic sensibilities. Adult eloquence, as I have suggested, assumes an ability to blend form and content—how something is said, in other words, is nearly as significant as what is said. On their way to mastery of this verbal eloquence, children explore the art of language expression through their play with humorous verse.

9 Parody Play

In the current social milieu, we are witnessing the burgeoning of the "low art" of parody. What is popular is anything, it seems, that comments disrespectfully on any and all aspects of life in America—or anywhere else, for that matter. In addition to the proliferation of things like "Off the Wall Street Journal" or "Not the New York Times" on newsstands, there are books entitled *How to Regain Your Virginity* and *Plain Jane Works Out* and even a white paperback called *Not the Bible*. TV has its own brand of spoofs with things like "Not Necessarily the News" and a mangled mini-series called "The Windy War." Finally, even something as stalwart and seemingly unfunny as the L. L. Bean catalogue has succumbed to the buffoonery of the current crop of humorists. For better or worse, we are in the midst of a veritable onslaught of attempts to poke fun through parody—the parody, that is, of overkill, outrageous exaggeration, and, more often than not, just plain bad taste. Scatological references, sexual slurs, and ethnic stereotyping through racial jokes are what too often motivate these attempts.

And in fact, though parody as a form of rhetoric has a long and respectable history, the current brand differs considerably from pieces produced just one or two generations ago. Then, such writers as S. J. Perelman, James Thurber, and Frank Sullivan, among others, applied the fine art of parodic sensibility—defined by close imitation of form and the introduction of calculated exaggeration—to reveal the anomalies and excesses found in parts of the literary, social, or political worlds. Unlike most of the current examples, these writers used parodic form for satirizing aspects of life. And it is, after all, the kind of critical thinking found in well-shaped satire, the kind that can be encouraged in the classroom, that can lead to useful and needed change.

A Developmental Perspective

Interestingly, the exploration of parody is not and has never been confined to the arena of adult humor. Children's oral language tradition has for generations included jokes and verses designed to poke fun. The rites of passage of the elementary ages are full of irreverences and the impulse to denigrate through verbal play. In their jokes and verses, children make fun of all they survey: themselves, their language, adults (especially teachers), and social conventions. As noted, one type of parody exploits differences among ethnic and religious groups. Examples of this type of humor, as I have argued, need to be examined in the context of a social studies program in which students have the opportunity to appreciate rather than denigrate differences among people and customs.

Other types of parody, however, reveal youngsters examining their own course of development. At seven and eight these young satirists take a hard look at themselves and their past. Now is the time, they seem to say, to put away childish things:

> Mary had a little lamb
> Her father shot it dead.
> It came with her to school one day
> Between two chunks of bread.

This is only one of the thirteen different parody versions of "Mary had a little lamb" that the Opies have recorded. As they point out, it is a truism of children's development that the most recently relinquished phase of growth receives the severest attack. In their wordplay, children deliver a fatal blow to "babyhood" by exercising their newly acquired verbal wit.

Children discover early that the quality of their lives is irrevocably determined by the powers that be—parents, teachers, and school. They comment—with unconcealed rancor—on these facts in a parody version of the "Battle Hymn of the Republic":

> My eyes have seen the glory
> Of the burning of the school,
> We have tortured all the teachers,
> We have broken all the rules.
> We will try to kill the principal tomorrow afternoon.
> His truth is marching on.

This example, I have found, continues to be "discovered" and savored by youngsters of eight or nine. By this age children have learned that authority is frequently expressed in the defining of "dos" and "don'ts." Accompanying this understanding is an awareness that, as children, they have a low place on the social hierarchy, an awareness for which such "subversive" wordplay might help to compensate.

As documented by Alleen Pace Nilsen (1983), children, like adult humorists, also indulge in scatology:

> I see London; I see France.
> I see Betsy's underpants.
> They aren't green, they aren't blue,
> They're just filled with number two . . .

as well as verses harboring sexual references:

> Jack and Jill went up the hill
> To fetch a pail of water.
> Jill forgot to take the pill
> And now she's got a daughter.

There are, of course, good developmental reasons for this. What we are witnessing are yet other examples of the expression of the socially inexpressible. Children are well aware that these areas of animal functioning are emotionally loaded and that the joke context provides a vehicle for sanctioning their expression. And, as noted, humorous verse absolves the speaker from some responsibility for what is said since the form—that is, rhyme and meter—must not be violated.

As Nilsen puts it, "If children should manage to grow up without being participators in, or at least spectators of, this kind of language play, they may miss out on learning cultural norms and attitudes relating to bodily functions and sexuality" (1983, 197). It seems, then, that such play functions to induct youngsters into acceptable social attitudes and behaviors in regard to these areas of living.

The Media Provide Mediums for Play

During my years of data collection for a study of children's verbal play in elementary classrooms (Geller 1981), I guided parody play sessions for a group of ten- and eleven-year-olds that produced hink-pinks related to their spelling/vocabulary studies. In one of the opportunities for play, the children were invited to create parody names of well-known products—"Belch's Grape Juice"—and TV shows—"The Si[c]k Million Dollar Man" (fig. 8). In previous years, some of these children had been introduced to this type of play through a product called "Wacky Pack" gum. The gum package contained trading cards on which appeared cartoon pictures of famous products, "Neveready Batteries," for example. The children were delighted by these cartoon cards and many had begun collections before the product was taken off the market because of lawsuits begun by irate companies.

Figure 8. "The Sik Million Dollar Man"

To begin this type of play, then, little more was required than to bring models of "Wacky Packs" to a group discussion period. After an examination of these, certain students began to create on the spot. Time spent in exploring examples, orally, was followed by chances to create on paper.

The students were not only eager to try out parody possibilities suggested by this model, they were also delighted by the cartoon format for presenting and sharing their creations. For play with products, the parody label was emblazoned on an illustration of the packaging material, while pictures to accompany parodies of TV titles depicted main characters in the attitudes suggested by the "new" version. Thus the demise of the once-powerful Six-Million-Dollar Man is amply elaborated in a drawing of a character whose nuts and bolts are flying every which way as he desperately attempts to prove himself on a running machine which registers "one mile per hour."

The students' play ranged, in approach, from the nonsensical to the genuinely critical and, thematically, from the scatological to the political. In those inventions derived more from nonsense than sense, the children reveled in multiple methods for constructing rhymes or pairing similar-sounding words: (1) "Drop-a-can of Orange Juice" (Tropicana Orange Juice); (2) "Goon's Eyes Shredded Feet" (Spoon Size Shredded Wheat); and (3) "The Toilet Zone, starring Flush Gordon" (the Twilight Zone). The substitution of similar-sounding words with different meanings in these contexts produces the desired absurdity.

Other creations exemplified play in which the parody versions offer a more direct criticism of attributes or typical reactions associated with the original. In this category belong the "Belch's Grape Juice" and the "Sik Million Dollar Man" examples. Others of this type are: (1) "Kung Fool" (Kung Fu); (2) "Newly Dead Game" (Newlywed Game); (3) "Die Pepsi" (Diet Pepsi); and (4) "Sun Pissed Oranges" (Sunkist Oranges).

At other times these students chose to play through the use of antonyms: "My-T-Bad" (My-T-Fine). While these examples do not exemplify the rules for parody in this model—similar in sound and syntax but different in meaning—they were nevertheless considered humorous by this group. Depending upon the sophistication of a particular elementary class, identification of parody "rules" could be stretched to include similarities of syntax with differences in sound and meaning.

These creations offer evidence for the readiness of ten- and eleven-year-olds to evaluate aspects of their culture and experience. Given these opportunities to play with name-phrases descriptive of nationally known products and television shows, youngsters poke fun by taking to task exaggerations and stereotypic views routinely employed in the promotion of these items. The media's consistent use of hyperbole and euphemism, the mixing of fact and fiction, is not overlooked by these ages. What seems to motivate their parodies is the obvious, if unintended, invitation to degrade items so described.

Finally, there were two inventions exemplary of a developing ability to use parodic form to satirize political elements of experience: (1) "Watergate Mental Creme, LSD, approved by Nixon" (Colgate Dental Creme, MFP, approved by dentists); and (2) "Green Tyrant German Style Sauerkraut" (fig. 9) (Green Giant sauerkraut). Some youngsters, then, are ready to construct and exploit humorous perspectives on what is current and topical. At this point in their growth, in fact, most students' developing awareness of the larger social world of which they are a part makes it possible to mobilize parodic impulses for the satirizing of social phenomena beyond the lacerating of peers and other purely "local" injustices. The student's play on "kraut" might motivate a discussion on nicknames often used for peers and sometimes for national groups, sometimes admiring, though frequently pejorative. Though never deliberately solicited in the classroom, such expressions, when they come up, give teachers an opportunity to explore and develop attitudes in students less prejudiced than those that lead to the formulation of such epithets.

In discussions of parody form, besides identifying and defining key sound/meaning patterns used in their inventions, these ages might be encouraged to articulate the nature of this type of humor:

> What are the differences/similarities between the forms of the parody and the original?
>
> What are the differences/similarities between their expressions of meanings?
>
> How does similarity in form combine with difference in meaning to make a humorous statement?
>
> How do you think the parody form makes its point?

Like other tasks in which teachers ask these ages to exercise critical thinking abilities, these discussion questions help to bring parody—a time-honored method for evaluating elements of experience—within the range of elementary school programs. As demonstrated, these ages are aware of the absurdity of much that is generally accepted as simply part of the culture, and opportunities to translate this absurdity into linguistic incongruities can strengthen this kind of thinking.

It was after my parody play sessions with this group that they began their study of medieval history. At the end of the school year, preparations for a dramatic presentation of their investigations were

Figure 9. "Green Tyrant German Style Sauerkraut"

begun. After some discussion, they decided—with their teacher's blessing—to create a series of skits poking fun at life in the "Muddled Ages." The students constructed scenes—"The Tournament," "The Feast," "The Cathedral," and "The Monastery"—in which the actions and possible motivations of characters of the age were irreverently explored. Depictions of incompetence of all sorts played a large part in these skits, as might be expected, since such incompetence lends itself so well to slapstick, a favorite form of children's humorous play.

Many of the satirical thrusts of each scene were expressed in lyrics accompanying the action. In "The Feast," verses about the nobleman's life (sung to the tune of "If I Were a Rich Man") describe what appears to be the obvious pleasures of being rich and powerful in these times:

> Wouldn't have to work hard
> 'Cause I'd have a thousand cooks
> And weavers, blacksmiths, minstrels, too.
> They would do the work around the place
> I would hunt and feed my face.

In the cathedral skit, the students described the major structural elements of this edifice in verses infused with sardonic humor (sung to the tune of "Yellow Submarine"):

> See the gargoyles way up high
> Catching water from the sky?
> When we walk beneath their spout
> They let the water all come out.
>
> Holding up this clumsy wall
> Stands the buttress very tall
> Flying buttresses in back
> Cause without 'em the walls would crack.

Finally, life in a monastery was brought under fire (sung to the tune of "Billy, Don't Be a Hero"):

> In the refectory, here's where we eat
> All our vegetable meals.
> Once a week, we eat meat
> And that's a big interesting deal.
> While eating it's always quiet
> And nobody ever says "Try it."
> Monasteries are merry only for monks
> And priests and abbots and novices . . .

In addition to their illustration of preadolescent wit, these verses offer evidence for the notion that to play with an idea requires a certain command of it. These satirical jibes derive from a fairly substantial knowledge of life in the Middle Ages. Further, in the parody about monks and monasteries, the students, as might be expected of these ages, find the asceticism of the lives of these people somewhat suspicious. Given the opportunity to evaluate ways of life—theirs alone or theirs in comparison to others'—these ages tend to take a level-headed view, describing a vision, one might say, which is neither unduly idealistic nor unremittingly cynical.

In this portrait of one class of ten- and eleven-year-olds, we have witnessed the beginnings of adult uses of parody. As students move into their junior and senior high school years, possibilities for parody can be expanded with little fear that the form might be used to abuse inappropriate targets. Students' growing alertness to social anomalies provides an endless source of material for play. A sense of citizenship begins to coalesce in the adolescent who discovers that the social systems that guide the lives of contemporary peoples, like those of their historical predecessors, are replete with inconsistencies, injustices, and even absurdities. Those elements of experience that bear critical examination are often neatly identified and highlighted in the multiple perspectives projected in parody play.

Conclusion: Times for Play

And as in uffish thought he stood,
  The Jabberwock, with eyes of flame,
Came whiffling through the tulgey wood,
  And burbled as it came!

One, two! One, two! And through and through
  The vorpal blade went snicker-snack!
He left it dead, and with its head
  He went galumphing back.

> —from "Jabberwocky," by Lewis Carroll

Blood and gore, rhyme and rhythm, new words born from old—Lewis Carroll delights both children and adults with his fanciful tale of the Jabberwock. Like others who practice the craft of poetry, Carroll is a master player with words. Shaping the sounds, stretching the meanings, alternating the lilt and crash, breaking the rules, and, sometimes, *making* the rules are activities that typify the poet at work with words. Language, the bards tell us, is never merely functional; it is expressive of feelings—or lack of them—depending upon the forms in which it is cast. And it is the poets who continually remind us that how something is said is as important as what is said.

Though not necessarily on the way to becoming poets, children explore the art of language in their wordplay. Developmentally, becoming a part of a community of people means that children come more and more to rely on this communication system. This is the medium through which they share feelings, thoughts, desires—all meaningful experience. To communicate these many aspects of life clearly requires a command of language's forms and functions. In their play children take time to scrutinize the system. Released for the moment from the need to get across the *what* of words, they examine the *how*. They hold up for view the building blocks of the system—its sounds, its meanings, its conventions, its capacity for humor as well as for hurt.

95

At the same time children explore boundaries of behavior. They test the limits of cultural "dos" and "don'ts" in the expression of subversive, often forbidden, sentiments.

In the past decade, a visible trend in research related to children's learning has been to support the significance of the whole in contrast to the parts of any given situation, to support the educational value of the entire context of the child's experiences rather than placing the usual stress upon decontextualized pieces. Within this framework, language learning, it is felt, whether through speaking, listening, reading, or writing, is optimal when it derives from experiences linking children's spontaneous interests and pursuits with demonstrated stages of language development. Most forms of verbal play practiced in the three-to-eleven age range provide just such an intersection of these aspects of child life.

All adults involved in the tender though trying task of educating children need to recognize that the intersection of emotional and intellectual responses in the teaching/learning moment is not just incidental—it is fundamental. Children, as Frank Smith (1981) puts it, are learning all the time. When they are exposed to the teaching of decontextualized skills—forms separated from the vitality lent by the aesthetic, humorous, and personally meaningful functions of language—they are learning that language education bears little relation to their lives and experiences. Worse, they are developing an attitude that the culture in which they will one day assume adult roles has little appreciation for meaningful communication. Those who survive this educational experience tend to do it despite rather than because of the skill-drill focus of many classroom language activities. The education of our young children needs to focus on keeping intact the wholeness of their response to life, and on learning through the exploration of language that is expressive of age-appropriate meanings, feelings, and ideas. In such a program, the many and varied uses of humorous wordplay would find a natural place.

References

Anisfeld, M. *Language Development from Birth to Three*. Hillsdale, N.J.: Lawrence Erlbaum Associates, 1984.

Bissex, G. L. *Gnys At Wrk: A Child Learns to Write and Read*. Cambridge: Harvard Univ. Press, 1980.

Britton, J. "Learning to Use Language in Two Modes." In *Symbolic Functioning in Childhood*, ed. N. R. Smith and M. B. Franklin. Hillsdale, N.J.: Lawrence Erlbaum Associates, 1979.

Brown, R. *A First Language: The Early Stages*. Cambridge: Harvard Univ. Press, 1973.

Burke, K. *A Grammar of Motives*. Englewood Cliffs, N.J.: Prentice-Hall, 1945.

Cassirer, E. *Language and Myth*. Trans. S. K. Langer. New York: Dover, 1953.

Cazden, C. B. *Child Language and Education*. New York: Holt, Rinehart & Winston, 1972.

Chukovsky, Kornei. *From Two to Five*. 1925. Reprint. Trans. and ed. Miriam Morton. Berkeley and Los Angeles: Univ. of California Press, 1971.

Chomsky, C. "Approaching Reading through Invented Spelling." In *Theory and Practice of Early Reading*, vol. 2, ed. L. B. Resnick and P. A. Weaver. Hillsdale, N.J.: Lawrence Erlbaum Associates, 1979.

Duckworth, E. "Either We're Too Early and They Can't Learn It or We're Too Late and They Know It Already: The Dilemma of 'Applying Piaget.'" *Harvard Educational Review* 4 (Aug. 1979): 297–312.

Fein, G. G., and N. Apfel. "Some Preliminary Observations on Knowing and Pretending." In *Symbolic Functioning in Childhood*, ed. N. R. Smith and M. B. Franklin. Hillsdale, N.J.: Lawrence Erlbaum Associates, 1979.

Ferguson, C. A., and M. A. Macken. "The Role of Play in Phonological Development." In *Children's Language*, vol. 4, ed. K. Nelson. Hillsdale, N.J.: Lawrence Erlbaum Associates, 1984.

Garvey, C. "Play with Language and Speech." In *Child Discourse*, ed. S. Ervin-Tripp and C. Mitchell-Kernan. New York: Academic Press, 1976.

———. *Play*. Cambridge: Harvard Univ. Press, 1977.

Geller, L. G. *Children's Humorous Language: A Curriculum for Developing Mastery of Verbal Skills*. Ph.D. diss., New York University, 1981.

Gleason, J. B. "Do Children Imitate?" Paper read at International Conference on Oral Education of the Deaf, Lexington School for the Deaf, 1967.

Goodman, K. S. "Celebrate Literacy." Presidential address to International Reading Association, Chicago, April, 1982.

Golomb, C. "Pretense Play: A Cognitive Perspective." In *Symbolic Functioning in Childhood*, ed. N. R. Smith and M. B. Franklin. Hillsdale, N.J.: Lawrence Erlbaum Associates, 1979.

Graves, D. *Balance the Basics: Let Them Write*. New York: Ford Foundation, 1978.

Henderson, E. H., and J. W. Beers, eds. *Developmental and Cognitive Aspects of Learning to Spell: A Reflection of Word Knowledge*. Newark, Del.: International Reading Association, 1980.

Herron, R. E., and B. Sutton-Smith, eds. *Child's Play: Collected Readings on the Biology, Ecology, Psychology and Sociology of Play*. New York: John Wiley & Sons, 1971.

Holdaway, D. *The Foundations of Literacy*. New York: Scholastic, 1979.

———. *Stability and Change in Literacy Learning*. Exeter, N.H.: Heinemann Educational Books, 1984.

Huizinga, J. *Homo Ludens: A Study of the Play Element in Culture*. Boston: Beacon Press, 1955.

Lakoff, G., and M. Johnson. *Metaphors We Live By*. Chicago: Univ. of Chicago Press, 1980.

Langer, S. K. *Philosophy in a New Key*. New York: New American Library, 1951.

Leopold, Werner F. *Speech Development of a Bilingual Child*. Evanston, Ill.: Northwestern Univ. Press, 1939–49. Reprint (vols. 6, 11, 18, and 19). New York: AMS, 1970.

Lieberman, I. Y. "Segmentation of the Spoken Word and Reading Acquisition." *Bulletin of the Orton Society* 23 (1973): 65–77.

McDowell, J. H. *Children's Riddling*. Bloomington: Indiana Univ. Press, 1979.

McGhee, P. "On the Cognitive Origins of Incongruity Humor: Fantasy Assimilation Versus Reality Assimilation." In *The Psychology of Humor*, ed. P. McGhee and J. Goldstein. New York: Academic Press, 1972.

Morris, D. "Concept of Word: A Developmental Phenomenon in the Beginning Reading and Writing Processes." *Language Arts* 58 (Sept. 1981): 659–68.

Nilsen, A. P. "Children's Multiple Uses of Oral Language Play." *Language Arts* 60 (Feb. 1983): 194–201.

Opie, I., and P. Opie. *The Lore and Language of Schoolchildren*. Oxford: Clarendon Press, 1959.

Pearson, P. D., and L. Fielding. "Research Update: Listening Comprehension." *Language Arts* 59 (Sept. 1982): 617–29.

Piaget, J. *Play, Dreams and Imitation in Childhood*. Trans. C. Gategno and F. M. Hodgson. New York: Norton, 1962.

Piaget, J., and Inhelder, B. *The Psychology of the Child*. Trans. H. Weaver. New York: Basic Books, 1969.

Read, C. *Children's Categorizations of Speech Sounds in English*. Urbana, Ill.: National Council of Teachers of English, 1975.

———. "Children's Awareness of Language, with Emphasis on Sound Systems." In *The Child's Conception of Language*, ed. A. Sinclair, R. J. Jarvella, and W. J. M. Levelt. New York: Springer-Verlag, 1978.

Rubin, Z. *Children's Friendships.* Cambridge: Harvard Univ. Press, 1980.

Sanches, M., and B. Kirshenblatt-Gimblett. "Children's Traditional Speech Play and Child Language." In *Speech Play,* ed. B. Kirshenblatt-Gimblett. Philadelphia: Univ. of Pennsylvania Press, 1976.

Schwartz, J. I. "Metalinguistic Awareness: A Study of Verbal Play in Young Children." Paper presented at the American Educational Research Association Conference, New York City, 1977. (ERIC/EECE ED 149 852.)

———. "Children's Experiments with Language." *Young Children* 36 (July 1981): 16–26.

Smith, F. "Making Sense of Reading—And of Reading Instruction." *Harvard Educational Review* 47 (Aug. 1977): 386–95.

———. "Conflicting Approaches to Reading Research and Instruction." In *Theory and Practice of Early Reading,* vol. 2, ed. L. B. Resnick and P. A. Weaver. Hillsdale, N.J.: Lawrence Erlbaum Associates, 1979.

Smith, N. R., and M. B. Franklin, eds. *Symbolic Functioning in Childhood.* Hillsdale, N.J.: Lawrence Erlbaum Associates, 1979.

Sutton-Smith, B. "A Developmental Structural Account of Riddles." In *Speech Play,* ed. B. Kirshenblatt-Gimblett. Philadelphia: Univ. of Pennsylvania Press, 1976.

Vygotsky, L. S. *Thought and Language.* 1934. Reprint. Trans. E. Hanfmann and G. Vakar. Cambridge: MIT Press, 1962.

Wolf, D., and H. Gardner. "Style and Sequence in Early Symbolic Play." In *Symbolic Functioning in Childhood,* ed. N. R. Smith and M. B. Franklin. Hillsdale, N.J.: Lawrence Erlbaum Associates, 1979.

Wolfenstein, M. *Children's Humor: A Psychological Study.* 1954. Reprint. Bloomington: Indiana Univ. Press, 1978.

Bibliography

This is only a small sampling of the many books exploring wordplay currently available for children. They are arranged by age groups for easy reference, though many may be useful and enjoyable for younger and/or older children.

The Nursery Years

Aldis, D. *All Together: A Child's Treasury of Verse*. New York: Putnam, 1952.

Anno, M. *Topsy-Turvies: Pictures to Stretch the Imagination*. New York: Weatherhill, 1970.

Barrett, J. *Animals Should Definitely Not Wear Clothes*. New York: Atheneum, 1970.

Berenstain, Stanley and Janice. *The Big Honey Hunt*. New York: Beginner, 1962.

Birmingham, J. *Mr. Grumpy's Outing*. New York: Holt, Rinehart & Winston, 1970.

Bodecker, N. *It's Raining Said John Twaining*. New York: Atheneum, 1973.

Brown, M. W. *Goodnight Moon*. New York: Harper & Row, 1947.

Copp, J. *Martha Matilde O'Toole*. Scarsdale, N.Y.: Bradbury Press, 1969.

de Angeli, M. *Book of Nursery and Mother Goose Rhymes*. New York: Doubleday, 1953.

Emberley, B. *Drummer Hoff*. Englewood Cliffs, N.J.: Prentice-Hall, 1967.

Fisher, A. *Cricket in a Thicket*. New York: Scribner's, 1963.

Hutchins, P. *The Surprise Party*. New York: Macmillan, 1969.

Kessler, E. *Do Baby Bears Sit on Chairs?* New York: Doubleday, 1961.

Krauss, R. *The Backward Day*. New York: Harper & Row, 1950.

———. *Bears*. New York: Harper & Row, 1948.

———. *I Can Fly*. New York: Golden Press, 1981.

Martin, Bill, Jr. *Sounds of Home*. Sounds of Language Readers Series. New York: Holt, Rinehart & Winston, 1966.

McLeod, E. *One Snail and Me*. Boston: Little, Brown, 1961.

McNaughton, C., and E. Attenborough. *Walk, Rabbit, Walk*. New York: Viking, 1977.

Ormerod, J. *Rhymes Around the Day*. New York: Penguin Books, 1983.

Quackenbush, R. *Old MacDonald Had a Farm*. Philadelphia: Lippincott, 1972.

———. *Go Tell Aunt Rody*. Philadelphia: Lippincott, 1973.

———. *Clementine*. Philadelphia: Lippincott, 1974.

———. *Pop Goes the Weasel and Yankee Doodle*. Philadelphia: Lippincott, 1976.

Tarrant, M. *Nursery Rhymes*. New York: Crowell, 1978.

Watson, Clyde. *Father Fox's Pennyrhymes*. New York: Crowell, 1971.

Wildsmith, Brian. *Brian Wildsmith's Mother Goose*. New York: Watts, 1965.

The Transition Years

Cerf, Bennett. *Book of Laughs*. Illus. Carl Rose. New York: Beginner, 1959.

——— . *Book of Riddles*. Illus. Ray McKie. New York: Beginner, 1960.

——— . *More Riddles*. Illus. Ray McKie. New York: Beginner, 1961.

——— . *Animal Riddles*. Illus. Ray McKie. New York: Beginner, 1963.

Martin, Bill, Jr. *Sounds around the Clock*. Sounds of Language Readers Series. New York: Holt, Rinehart & Winston, 1966.

Milne, A. A. *Winnie-the-Pooh*. 1926. Reprint. New York: E. P. Dutton, 1957.

——— . *The House at Pooh Corner*. 1928. Reprint. New York: E. P. Dutton, 1957.

Seuss, Dr. *And to Think That I Saw It on Mulberry Street*. New York: Vanguard, 1937.

Tarrant, Margaret. *Nursery Rhymes*. New York: Crowell, 1978.

Withers, Carl. *A Rocket in My Pocket*. Illustrated by William Wiesnes. New York: Scholastic, 1975.

The Middle Elementary Years

Aardema, Verna. *Ji-Nongo-Nongo: Means Riddles*. Illustrated by Jerry Pinkney. New York: Four Winds Press, 1978.

Bruce, Dana, ed. *Tell Me a Riddle*. Illustrated by Frank Elkin. New York: Platt & Munk, 1966.

Carroll, Lewis. *Alice's Adventures in Wonderland*. New York: Delacorte, 1966.

——— . *Through the Looking Glass*. New York: Grosset & Dunlap, 1946.

Doty, Roy. *Puns, Gags, Quips and Riddles: A Collection of Dreadful Jokes*. Garden City, N.Y.: Doubleday, 1974.

Emrich, Duncan, ed. *The Hodgepodge Book, Containing All Manner of Curious, Interesting and Out-of-the-Way Information Drawn from American Folklore, and Not To Be Found Anywhere Else in the World; As Well As Jokes, Conundrums, Riddles, Puzzles and Other Matter Designed to Amuse and Entertain: All of It Most Instructive and Delightful*. Illustrated by Ib Ohlsson. New York: Four Winds, 1972.

Juster, Norton. *The Phantom Tollbooth*. Illustrated by Jules Feiffer. New York: Random House, 1972.

Kohl, Marguerite, and Frederica Young. *Jokes for Children*. Illus. Bob Patterson. New York: Hill and Wang, 1963.

McGovern, Ann, ed. *Barrel of Chuckles*. Illustrated by Allen Jaffe. New York: Scholastic, 1960.

Martin, Bill, Jr. *Sounds of a Distant Drum*. Sounds of Language Readers Series. New York: Holt, Rinehart & Winston, 1967.

O'Neill, Mary. *Words, Words, Words*. Illustrated by Judy Piussi-Campbell. Garden City, N.Y.: Doubleday, 1966.

Sarnoff, Jane, and Reynold Ruffins. *The Monster Riddle Book*. New York: Scribner's, 1978.

Schwartz, Alvin, ed. *A Twister of Twists, A Tangler of Tongues*. Illustrated by Glen Rounds. Philadelphia: Lippincott, 1973.

———, ed. *Tomfoolery: Trickery and Foolery with Words*. Illustrated by Glen Rounds. Philadelphia: Lippincott, 1973.

———, ed. *Cross Your Fingers, Spit in Your Hat, Superstitions and Other Beliefs*. Illus. Glen Rounds. Philadelphia: Lippincott, 1974.

———, ed. *Whoppers, Tall Tales and Other Lies*. Illustrated by Glen Rounds. Philadelphia: Lippincott, 1975.

———, ed. *Witcracks: Jokes and Jests from American Folklore*. Illustrated by Glen Rounds. Philadelphia: Lippincott, 1973.

Steig, William. *C D B!* New York: Windmill Books and E. P. Dutton, 1968.

Stoutenburg, Adrien. *American Tall Tales*. New York: Viking, 1966.

———. *American Tall-Tale Animals*. Illustrated by Glen Rounds. New York: Viking, 1968.

Tripp, Wallace, editor and illustrator. *A Great Big Ugly Man Came Up and Tied His Horse to Me*. Boston: Little, Brown, 1973.

Troop, Miriam, editor and illustrator. *The Limerick Book Collection of Riddles, Puns, Tongue Twisters*. New York: Grosset & Dunlap, Inc., 1976.

Weigle, Oscar, ed. *Great Big Joke and Riddle Book*. Illustrated by Crosby Bonsall, John Huehnergarth, Susan Perl and Bill and Bonnie Rutherford. New York: Grosset & Dunlap, 1970.

Books about Language for the Middle Elementary Years

Adelson, Leone. *Dandelions Don't Bite*. Illustrated by Lou Myers. New York: Pantheon Books, 1972.

Epstein, Sam and Beryl. *The First Book of Words*. New York: Watts, 1954.

Ernst, Margaret S. *Words, English Roots and How They Grow*. New York: Knopf, 1957.

Helfman, Elizabeth. *Signs and Symbols Around the World*. New York: Lothrop, Lee & Shepard, 1965.

Kraske, Robert. *The Story of the Dictionary*. New York: Harcourt Brace Jovanovich, 1975.

Laird, Helene and Charlton. *The Tree of Language*. Illustrated by Ervine Metzl. New York: World Publishing, Times, Mirror, 1972.

Longman, Harold. *What's Behind the Word?* New York: Coward-McCann, 1968.

Matthews, Mitford. *American Words*. Illustrated by Lorence Bjorklund. Cleveland: Williams Collins and World Publishing Company, Inc., 1976.

Nurnberg, Maxwell. *Wonder in Words*. Illustrated by Frederick W. Turton. Englewood Cliffs, N.J.: Prentice-Hall, 1968.

All Ages

Bodecker, N. M. *Let's Marry Said the Cherry, and Other Nonsense Poems*. New York, Atheneum, 1974.

Ciardi, John. *The Reason for the Pelican.* Illustrated by Madeleine Gekiere. New York: J. B. Lippincott, 1959.

Clymer, Eleanor, ed. *Arrow Book of Funny Poems.* Illustrated by Doug Anderson. New York: Scholastic, 1961.

Cole, William, ed. *Beastly Boys and Ghastly Girls.* Illustrated by Tomi Ungerer. New York: World Publishing, 1964.

———, ed. *Oh, What Nonsense!* Illustrated by Tomi Ungerer. New York: Viking, 1969.

De Regniers, Beatrice Schenck, Eva Moore and Mary Michaels White, eds. *Poems Children Will Sit Still For: A Selection for the Primary Grades.* New York: Citation, 1969.

Einsel, W. *Did You Ever See?* New York: Scholastic, 1962.

Emrich, Duncan, ed. *The Nonsense Book of Riddles, Rhymes, Tongue Twisters, Puzzles and Jokes from American Folklore.* Illustrated by Ib Ohlsson. New York: Four Winds, 1970.

Gwynne, Fred. *A Chocolate Moose for Dinner.* New York: Windmill Books and E. P. Dutton, 1975.

———. *The King Who Rained.* New York: Windmill Books and E. P. Dutton, 1970.

Hoberman, Mary Ann. *A Little Book of Little Beasts.* Illustrated by Peter Parnall. New York: Simon & Schuster, 1973.

———. *The Raucous Auk: A Menagerie of Poems.* Illustrated by Joseph Low. New York: Viking, 1973.

Jacobs, Leland B., ed. *Poetry for Chuckles and Grins.* Illustrated by Tomie de Paola. Champaign, Ill.: Garrard, 1968.

Langstaff, John, and Carol Langstaff, eds. *Shimmy Shimmy Coke-Ca-Pop! A Collection of City Children's Street Games and Rhymes.* Photographs by Don MacSorley. Garden City, N.Y.: Doubleday, 1973.

Parrish, Peggy. *Amelia Bedelia.* Illustrated by Fritz Siebel. New York: Scholastic, 1963.

———. *Thank You, Amelia Bedelia.* Illustrated by Fritz Siebel. New York: Harper & Row, 1964.

———. *Amelia Bedelia and the Surprise Shower.* Illustrated by Fritz Siebel. New York: Scholastic, 1966.

———. *Come Back, Amelia Bedelia.* Illustrated by Wallace Tripp. New York: Scholastic, 1971.

———. *Play Ball, Amelia Bedelia.* Illustrated by Wallace Tripp. New York: Scholastic, 1972.

Thaler, Mike. *Magic Letter Riddles.* New York: Scholastic, 1974.